HOLISTIC PSYCHOLOGY OF ALEXANDER PINT

LOVE – HATE

HOW TO DEAL WITH CONFLICTS IN PERSONAL RELATIONSHIPS

By ALEXANDER PINT

Translated by Emin Kuliev, MD

www.pint.ru

https://caterpillartobuterfly.wordpress.com

skyrocket press

Visit www.SkyrocketPress.com

Cover art by Freydoon Rassouli
ISBN: 978-1-944722-04-3

Close personal relationships give birth to the most serious problems and conflicts of our life. How can we get out of the dead end of recurrent conflicts and avoid the nervous breakdowns and diseases produced by them?

This book reviews the questions that bother every human being in a dialogue format. What are the real reasons that stand behind the misunderstanding between husbands and wives, parents and children, friends and relatives? How can we eliminate them and obtain harmony in our inner and outer worlds? How can we connect the energy of our thoughts, desires, and feelings and realize our aims? What will allow us to combine our common interests with our individual interests?

This book discusses these and many other questions using practical examples.

TABLE OF CONTENTS

•◦•◦•◦•◦•◦•◦•◦•◦•◦•◦•◦•◦•◦•◦•

Duality "LOVE—HATE"
OR HOW TO LIVE PEACEABLY WITH THE PEOPLE WHO ARE CLOSE TO YOU

CHAPTER 1
HOW TO FREE YOURSELF OF NEGATIVE EMOTIONS

•◆•◆•◆•◆•◆•◆•◆•◆•◆•◆•◆•◆•◆•◆•◆•◆•◆•

Your joy is your sorrow unmasked.
And the selfsame well from which your laughter rises was oftentimes filled with your tears.
And how else can it be?
The deeper that sorrow carves into your being, the more joy you can contain.
Is not the cup that holds your wine the very cup that was burned in the potter's oven?
And is not the lute that soothes your spirit, the very wood that was hollowed with knives?
When you are joyous, look deep into your heart and you shall find it is only that which has given you sorrow that is giving you joy.
When you are sorrowful look again in your heart, and you shall see that in truth you are weeping for that which has been your delight.
Some of you say, "Joy is greater than sorrow," and others say, "Nay, sorrow is the greater."

But I say unto you, they are inseparable.
Together they come, and when one sits alone with you at your board, remember that the other is asleep upon your bed. Verily you are suspended like scales between your sorrow and your joy.
Only when you are empty are you at standstill and balanced.
When the reassure-keeper lifts you to weigh his gold and his silver, needs must your joy or your sorrow rise or fall.

— Khalil Gibran, *The Prophet, On Joy and Sorrow*

Why and how negative emotions appear

— What kind of emotions do you and the people around you experience most frequently?

— *Fear, irritation…*

— How do people who fight other people feel? We frequently see these scenes on TV and in our daily lives. Do they experience happiness or fear? Would people pick up guns and shoot other people if they were happy? What do you think people who fight for power feel?

— *Envy, aggression.*

— What do people who stand in line experience?

— *They are tired and impatient.*

— What did your parents feel during your last meeting?

— *I think they felt some kind of disappointment with life. They were unsure of themselves.*

— What do you talk about when you meet with your friends? Do you discuss how beautiful your day was?

— *No, usually we do not.*

— If we were to take a look at ourselves and the people around us, we would see the display of many negative emotions. We can ask ourselves this question: Did we come to Earth only to be constantly dissatisfied and to experience suffering, or perhaps was this world given to us for some other purpose? How many genuinely happy people do we see in our lives? How often do we feel happy? Why do we experience negative emotions? Are they necessary?

— *Negative emotions represent our reactions to certain events.*

— Where is the root cause of these reactions?

— *We frequently depend on other people and circumstances, or other people depend on us. We constantly want to get something from our husbands, wives, children, employees, etc. When we do not get what we want, we experience irritation and anger.*

— It follows, then, that our dependencies are the reason for negative emotions. A lot comes from childhood. When a child is born he needs a lot, but he cannot do much on his own. He needs food, shelter, toys, and attention. How can he get it? How can a small child get what he needs?

— *He can get it from his parents.*

— What if a child is happy and laughs all the time. Will parents pay attention to such a child?

— *No.*

— And what if a child screams and cries, demanding what he wants. Will they run to him? A child might be left alone, but it is a rare mother who would leave her child for long. What does a child do when he wets himself? He starts to scream. A child develops a certain **mechanism of behavior** in relationship to the outside world that helps him to receive what he wants. A small child depends on other people. Do you think a child feels this dependency?

— *No.*

— No? Have you seen a child who wants something badly? Have you seen kids throwing tantrums in the supermarkets and screaming "I want ice-cream!" A mother, upon whom this purchase depends, thinks, "Okay. I do not want to deal with this now. I will buy whatever he wants." Two years later, he throws a tantrum asking for a scooter. Then he throws a tantrum asking for a car, and twenty years later—for his wife to do something for him. He develops a certain **stereotypical mechanism of behavior**. He understands that in order to get something, he needs to throw a tantrum. Another child may develop the opposite stereotype of behavior. He may cry quietly in the corner waiting for someone to come and help him to do what he needs. One child is aggressive. He breaks everything around him and demands to be given what he wants. Another gets what he wants using pity. The stereotypical mode of behavior we have acquired to get something from our parents manifests itself in our adult life now. Have you thought about that? Have you noticed that? Recall how you got what you wanted when you were five years old. If you don't remember, ask your parents.

Were you an obedient child? Obedience is another method to get what you want.

Do you know what unconditional love is?

— Do you know what unconditional love is? Have you experienced love that is not been conditioned on anything? Few of us experienced unconditional love in childhood. Most parents constantly demand something from their children. Even if you were lucky to be loved for just being here, there were people around you who did not love you for who you were. You had teachers. Even if they loved you, they probably did not love you for your own sake. In school and at home, love is a bargain, a business transaction. "I will love you if you do this for me." A child learns this very well. He starts to understand that for him to deserve mom's love, i.e. for her to do what he needs—to buy something for him or to take care of him—he needs to be quiet and obedient, or to scream and cry. He needs to do something to which mom usually reacts. Mom tells him, "Be a good boy. Behave yourself. Don't get your pants dirty. Don't play with that good-for-nothing neighbor boy. Study well and bring home good grades." That's how this business transaction called "mutual love" is made and maintained on both sides. The conditions are clearly defined: "You are good if ..." This is what conditioned love is. That's why most people can only love themselves and others in exchange for something. But is this really love? Most people simply don't know what love is, even though they use this word frequently. In reality, what they call love is just a business arrangement. A wife tells her husband, "I will love you if you..." He replies, "Okay, but you will have to ..."

So, what does this interesting word "love" reflect? It reflects the conditions of the business arrangement. **Love is a notion we use to manipulate other people in order to satisfy our own egoistic desires.** This is a very sly manipulation. A human being, who does not even know what love is, wants to be loved and is afraid to lose love. Usually a groom and a bride try to show themselves from their best sides. However, bride and wife, as well as groom and husband are the same people. The only difference between them is that the initial manipulation between them is very light; with time, it gets heavier and heavier. Eventually, masks are taken off. Both husband and wife understand that initially they have to be caring. "I will make it as pleasant as I can for you. I will show you how I can love now. The bill will come later. But you will have to pay for this love." Eventually, this truth becomes obvious for both of them. This is the nature of the arrangement. Men and women do it equally well. Every one of us learned how to do this in childhood.

We were taught to see the world as a dangerous place, where we must take care of ourselves. Nobody will give us anything for free. A human being learns these notions during early childhood when, in order to get something, a child needs to manipulate his relatives. Children learn the technique of manipulation from their parents very fast. Conditioned love is an arrangement. Unconditional love is a big secret that practically no one knows about—I love you the way you are. Is there anyone in your life who you love the way he or she is?

— *I love my child the way he is.*

— What do you mean when you tell him, "You have to do this and that"? Do you use these words when you talk to him? Do you get upset with him?

— *It is hard not to get upset with a child.*

— It is not hard. It can be done. It is nauseating to be unhappy, and it is great to be happy. It's a hard to be unhappy. It is hard to manipulate people. It is hard because it is unnatural. Whatever is natural is not hard. Try to run sideways and jump every fourth step.

— *It is uncomfortable.*

— Yes, it is uncomfortable, but that is how most people go through life, instead of running around happily.

How dependencies appear, and how they manifest themselves

— Where do we get all our dependencies? They are transmitted to us genetically and through our upbringing. How do our parents bring us up? How does society influence our upbringing? What does a child see and hear when he watches TV? What kinds of thoughts are being introduced to him? "Eat a Snickers Bar and be happy!" "Get admitted to a prestigious college and you will succeed in life. You will make a lot of money. You will be happy!" "You will get married, give birth to children, and be happy." A small human being listens to all of this and believes what adults tell him. When he grows up, he knows who is who and what is what. He knows what to strive for and why he should strive for it. He thinks, feels, and behaves the way he was taught to think, feel, and behave as a child. If he was told that he can get things only by using force, this conviction is ingrained in him. It becomes self-obvious to him. He does not doubt it. When he needs something, he demands and threatens others. He might think about which car to buy or where he should go for a vacation, but he does not have to think how to make another human being do what he wants him to do. He already knows everything: he needs to scream, to cry, or to scare him with a gun. He has learned this mechanism as a child. His program works in him like a clock, even though he is not aware of it. He turned into a robot that thinks, feels, and acts based on a certain program. He already knows everything. He knows how to be "happy." He knows how to manipulate other people. He knows how to behave in any situation. If all these programs were correct, we would be living in a society of happy people. But is that the case? Do we see many happy people around us? No. Looks like these programs are not working. Nevertheless, people continue to operate based on them. Why? Why do they do things that don't bring them happiness?

Scientists performed an interesting experiment. They put a hungry rat into a maze. There were ten tracks in the maze. A piece of cheese was positioned in the middle of the fourth track. The rat, after running down different tracks, found cheese on the fourth track. From then on, it would run straight to the cheese using track number four; it knew where to look for food. Two weeks later scientists moved the cheese to track number ten. What did the rat do? It habitually ran down the fourth track, but it did not find cheese there. It returned, sat on the crossroad for a while, and ran down the same track again. The rat did it five times. Eventually, the rat started to explore other tracks and finally found the cheese.

What does a human being do in a similar situation? He continues to run down the path from which cheese was removed for the rest of his life. For example, a politician always says what his electorate wants to hear from him. What does he get at the end? He gets a heart attack and pangs of conscience. He gets everything but happiness. He achieved what he wanted to achieve, but he is broken inside. He maintained his image all his life. He honored moral obligations and duty. What did he finally come to? He came to realize the fact that he does not need such a life. He reached the top as a politician, but as a human being, he crashed. How many lives of a Hitler or Stalin quality does one need to experience to understand that power does not lead to happiness? Power is a very attractive piece of cheese for many people. Many strive for this piece of cheese, but when they get it, they soon become nauseated by it.

So, what happens? It looks like we have many negative emotions in our life. These negative emotions point to our main dependencies. A man comes to a psychologist and says, "I am stressed out. I am constantly irritated. I feel bad. Please, help me." The psychologist starts to work with his emotions, asks him to breathe a certain way, count to hundred when he gets anxious, etc. This calms our man down for a while. Then he goes to work and sees his boss. His blood pressure goes up, and he runs back to the psychologist, who says, "Okay, let's do some more breathing exercises, and try a new massage." He comes home afterwards, sees his wife, and starts to tremble inside.

We must search for the root cause of things, i.e. we have to recognize our dependencies. **A negative emotion is just an indicator of these dependencies**. Do you need negative emotions? Do you need jealousy, irritation, and envy?

— *Perhaps we need them for comparison. Perhaps we need them to know that there are other, more pleasant states.*

— Then what do we need poor people for? Do we need them for rich people to know that they are rich? What do we need men for? Do we need men for women to know that they are women? Everything here is reciprocal. A woman considers herself a real woman when she is surrounded by real men. However, she constantly needs to prove to herself and to others that she is a real woman. She needs to constantly confirm her status and to pass the qualification test. A man who considers himself a real man also needs to pass the qualification test, for example, by going to the gym for three hours a day, making money, etc. He is surrounded by women who scream, "You are a real man!" while he throws money at them. You must pay for everything. To feel yourself as a real woman, you must pay. To feel yourself as a real man, you must pay. You must pay for every kaif* here. (* to the bottom of the page ... Kaif or Kif - from Arabic kayf pleasure. Any drug or agent that, when smoked, is capable of producing a euphoric condition. The euphoric condition produced by smoking marijuana.)

Do you experience negative emotions in connection to being a woman?

— *I do encounter situations when my being a woman is a hindrance. My boss told me yesterday, "What kind of logical thoughts can you have if you are a woman?"*

— Yes, but at the same time, that's where your so-called woman's advantage lies. A man who approaches you in the park and tries to strike up a conversation with you will behave differently in the office. He feels humiliated in the park, and he feels powerful in the office. Do you understand that this is the same thing? To be a real woman and to be a real man is the same dependency.

— *Can one get rid of all his dependencies?*

— Yes. However, you must understand the mechanism of their appearance first. What is dependency? **Behind every dependency is the expectations we have of life, the frustration of which leads to strong negative emotions.** What are the usual causes that lead people to experience strong negative emotions? Some people do not even allow themselves to express them fully. They suppress them. That leads to boredom and indifference. You must allow yourself to manifest them. Allow yourself to feel when, where, and with whom you experience them. **Every negative emotion is an indicator of your dependency**. If you want to rid yourself of negative emotions, you must work with the root causes of them, i.e. work with the dependencies that are behind them. You need to find and see these dependencies clearly.

Behind negative emotions lie dependencies of which you need to become aware. Yesterday you were upset with the economic and political situation in the country. You said, "I am Okay, but this country is going under." In reality, you are experiencing a very strong fear for your own wellbeing and are projecting your dependency onto the entire country. What about the country in which you are living does not satisfy you? What is so bad about it? What kind of emotions does this situation cause you to have?

— *I am **irritated** by the fact that our science was destroyed. I am a scientist, and that is what upsets me the most. There are no opportunities for a scientist at home. Scientists go abroad. Nobody needs me as a specialist here anymore.*

— Here you go. This is your dependency. You are afraid of becoming useless. That is why the situation with science concerns you so much. **Behind every strong negative emotion that you experience always hides your dependency.** Something happens in the world in a way you don't want to happen.

Notions about life instead of life

What is dependency? Dependency is a template. I apply such a template and I say, "Something is not right here. Something does not match here," and I start to experience fear, irritation, jealousy, or another negative emotion. I apply my template to another human being and say, "Nothing matches here at all. Oh my God?! You are so bad; how could I have married you? You turned out not to be who I expected you to be. You have screwed up my whole life." **Behind every**

dependency there is always some kind of a template, "You should be tall, but you are short. You should make a lot of money, but you do not. You should love children, but you do not. I spent my whole life on you, but you…"

He is just the way he is, but your image, or your template of him is different. When you superimpose your template on him, you see that he is not what you expect him to be, and you feel irritation.

You wake up and you want to go to the beach, but instead of the sunny Sunday you expected, you see rain. You say, "How horrible. The whole day is ruined." Your template presupposes sun, but reality offers you rain. You expected to see handsome guys on the beach, but you cannot even go there. This is the end. Life does not fit your template, and that makes you unhappy. You spend your entire day upset at the world. You ruin your entire day and make everyone around you miserable because your expectations have not been met. This is dependency. Those are the templates and stereotypes with which we approach our wives, husbands, children, coworkers, and life situations. We superimpose a certain template on a human being and expect him to match this stereotype. But that cannot happen because life is fluid. Life changes all the time, while the template we bring from the past is dead. Life does not match your template, and that leads you to experience negative emotions. Those templates want to oppress life. We apply our personal templates to life, but life does not correspond to them. Why should it? If life were to correspond to people's templates, it would not be life anymore; it would be hell. We create this hell ourselves perceiving life through our habitual stereotypes. The mechanism to make yourself unhappy is simple—you just need to demand something.

Another way to behave is to accept everything life gives you. In this case, you might say, "We are going to have a great day at the beach today. I love rain. We are going to swim under the rain."

You love the sun and you love the rain. You accept what life gives you today with gratitude. For this to happen, you need to learn to see your dependencies and templates. Let us start seeing our dependencies and let us free ourselves from them. I invite you to start to work as a self-investigator. When you start self-investigating constantly, your life changes, it becomes much more interesting.

Start freeing yourself from dependencies connected to safety, pleasure, and power. Set up this aim for yourself. These dependencies force you to manipulate other people. If you want to get something from another human being and he does not want to give it to you, you must force him. People usually see the world as good when it satisfies all their dependencies. Since we have many dependencies, we start to manipulate others in order to get what we think we need.

In essence, every human being strives for love. However, most of us can "love" another human being only if he does something we expect him to do. "You have to do this for me. You have to do that for me. I will love you if you do that for me."

Why do we need to free ourselves from our dependencies? Because they do not allow us to get pleasure out of life, to feel its fullness. Are there any good dependencies? Perhaps you might say that you have some good dependencies that do not cause you to have negative emotions. Let us say that one of your dependencies is to have a lot of money. A human being who wants to have a lot of money is very unhappy. He constantly tries to fool others. When he finally gets his money, he still cannot be happy, since now he is constantly worried about how not to lose what he has and how to get more of it.

Another example is a man who "loves" women. He has to constantly seek, court, and compete for women. Is he happy? No. He experiences certain pleasurable moments, but then he returns to the endless pursuit of pleasure. He is constantly running from himself. In this endless chase, a human being forgets something very important. He forgets himself. Alcoholics cannot stop and look at the world through sober eyes, because the reality they will see would scare them. The pursuit of pleasure is nothing but an escape. We escape to forget ourselves in something *pleasant*, and the harder the life circumstances, the harder we try to forget ourselves.

Can you run away from pain?

— To run away from pain is to not understand yourself. A human being wants to get rid of pain. You can do that, but only for a short period. It will catch up with you until you stop and think about the reason this pain appeared. **Why was this particular disease or accident given to you?** Why did life specifically order that ordeal for you rather than something else? Stop and think, and you will not step on the same rake twice. You had a fight with your wife, do not rush to divorce her. Your next partner will be the same; the situation will repeat itself. You were insulted. Try not to retaliate or scream. Think. You can get out of this uncomfortable situation by using a little bit of awareness. To do that, you need to change your perception about the event. You can do this if you have not yet been totally sucked into the swamp of your personal dependencies.

Do we think about how to prevent disease, an accident, or a betrayal? Do we think how not to slip on ice? We must be observant and attentive. Yet we run on ice not noticing that it is getting thinner and thinner under our feet. We fall, and we curse everyone around us for our own carelessness. We criticize and condemn our spouses, friends, and colleagues for some minor wrongdoings while failing to see how we provoked them to behave that way. We provoke life to treat us harshly. We are egoists. We scream that life does not provide us with what we think we deserve. However, do we really deserve what we want? Do we notice that life, which is very smart, gives us a lot of happiness? No, we do not see that. We pay attention to and remember every harsh word said to us, but we forget the words of gratitude and love. As a result, the world appears to be unkind and cruel to us. The unkindness and cruelty lives in our hearts, but we don't want to admit that. How often do we step into another man's shoes and try to understand him better? Not often. So, do we want to live in the world of love, or in the jungles of our own fears? We should become aware of what we want, and take a step on the path we have chosen. Let us not talk about those who have chosen the jungle, as only death will stop them. Let us join those who want to live in the world of love and happiness. It is difficult to be happy in a world filled with so much cruelty and anger, but it is possible. Let us help each other on this journey.

— *Some dependencies are considered acceptable, and society even views them as good. Is there such a thing as a good dependency?*

— A Buddhist would say that we don't need anything but a spoonful of rice, a shirt and a pair of pants to keep us warm, and a roof over our heads. Students of Buddhism have strong dependency on this conviction. They say, "I will not depend on anything" and then proceed to depend on this conviction.

If a human being has a free choice, everything makes him happy. This is probably the most beautiful thing here. When we refuse something in the name of something else, we are not free. By the way, dependency is not only a strong desire, it is also a strong disinclination. Is there something in your life that you strongly do not want to do or to have?

— *Yes.*

— There are people who say, "I don't want anything." These people have many things and situations that they strongly do not want to have.

For example, you do not want people to be in your way, or you do not want to communicate with someone. These are also dependencies. Both a strong desire and a strong disinclination are attempts to narrow down and to constrict life. Life is a river to which you say, "You should not run here. You should run over there, and you should run slower."

Who are we to tell life what to do? Life knows what to do. Yet, most of us try to order life around.

In order to liberate yourself from dependencies, you will have to change your views on life. For example, you have a strong dependency on your work and your boss. Does it mean that in order to free yourself of these dependencies you need to quit your work? You are strongly dependent on a certain man or a woman. Does it mean you need to stop seeing him or her? Not necessarily. The most important thing here is to change your relationship with the situation and people around you. When we change our inner world, we change our external environment, not vice versa. This is not a manipulation. A manipulator tries to adjust the external world to fit his dependencies. As that cannot be done, he experiences very difficult times. We, on the other hand, change the external world by working with our inner worlds. When I change my relationship with certain things and to certain events, I start to see them differently. They don't upset me anymore. They may even make me happy. We change our perception of life, not life itself.

In the grip of pleasure and power

Let us talk about our dependencies on pleasure. These dependencies are more characteristic for the societies with a higher level of economic development. For example, many westerners have many dependencies on pleasure, while constant economic instability in Russia strengthens its people's dependency on security. A higher level of economic development led to a fixation on pleasure in the West: where am I going to spend my Sunday, which car am I going to drive, which club am I to attend? A developed consumer society offers many pleasures that reinforce people's dependencies on them. However, if your business is to go down, you may lose your house, your car, and the comfort you have gotten used to. For those who are in the habit of having this comfort, it is hard to refuse it. It is much more difficult for them to refuse it than for those who are not in the habit of having it. Many women and quite a few men face this problem nowadays. For example, a woman lives with a man who provides her with a certain level of comfort for which she is paying one way or another. What does she get at the end? On one hand, she feels that she is not free, and that nothing she has is what she wants, but on the other hand, she is afraid to lose it. She says, "I am bored with everything. I feel like I am in jail." However, when an opportunity presents itself for her to leave, and this opportunity is always present, she does not grab it. Why? First, she is afraid to be alone. Second, she does not want to lose her habitual comfort: nice apartment, good car, and expensive outings and vacations. A habit has been formed in her. This is a big dependency for which a human being pays the highest price—his freedom. We must pay for everything here.

Our next dependency is our desire for power. This is a very strong dependency. Some types of power are easily visible. For example, the fight for power is easily visible in politics where competing parties fight each other. But the fight for power is present everywhere. You may say, "I am not after power. I don't need it." However, you may notice yourself raising your voice while talking to another human being, or talking very quietly to him. What is this? Is it a fight for power? While being in the company of other people, you may behave in a certain way that brings attention to you. What is that if not a fight for power? Let us go further. Every dependency creates an illusory perception of the surrounding world. A human being who has dependencies does not see reality; he only sees things that correspond to his stereotypical requirements. How will a man see the world who is oriented toward power? He will pay attention to those he must fight, who prevent him from achieving his personal goals, or to those he can use to achieve his goals. Nothing else is of interest to him. When he looks at something, he looks at it from the standpoint of how useful or harmful it is for him.

What would a man see who is oriented to receive pleasure? He will only see what offers him an opportunity to receive pleasure. If a man is concerned with safety, he will see everything from a possible danger point of view: is it dangerous for me or not, can I protect myself from it or not? Can these people see life, people, and events around them the way they really are? No. They see everything through the prism of their dependencies.

A man who has dependencies cannot see holistically; the more dependencies he has, the narrower his vision. He does not see the world the way it is; he sees it distorted by his dependencies. He sees a distorted, illusory world. People who strive after power will say that the world is a constant fight. People who strive after security will say that the world is full of dangers.

But the world just reflects us like a mirror. Few people see the world the way it really is. They see it the way they are at that moment. If a man is afraid, he sees danger in everyone and everything. He sees the manifestation of himself, i.e. of his own fears in everything that surrounds him.

The way to get rid of your dependencies

How can you free yourself from your dependencies? To do that, you need to see them and understand how they force you to manipulate other people by running your life and lives of the people next to you. Once you start to see your dependencies, you will realize that you do not need them. You must see them. You must realize that they turn your life and the lives of those next to you into hell.

For example, you take your child to the zoo. If you are fixated on safety, you will only see the animals that can bite you or your child. You may pay attention to someone who you think might rob you. It is a beautiful zoo. Different animals have been gathered there, but if you are fixated on the notion of safety, you will only be concerned with being robbed or bitten. That is what happens to you in every situation, everywhere, all the time.

If you are oriented to receive pleasure, you will look at the monkeys, who … and think… There is only one thing in your head in that case. Perhaps to think of sex is more pleasurable than to think of danger all day long, but this is quite a limiting point of view too.

A man oriented on power will look at the elephant and think, "Look how big he is. I want to be as powerful and important as this elephant."

Choose one dependency you are ready to part with. Look at how it distorts your perception of yourself and the people around you. What can you see through the prism of your dependencies, and what can't you see?

The world is a mirror that reflects me. When I don't see my dependencies, I project them onto other people and see my problems in every one of them.

So, how does a given dependency distort your perception? Take the man who irritates you the most. What do you see in him now, and what could you see in him if you were to free yourself from the dependency that prevails in your perception of this human being? Do this experiment right now.

Use any opportunity life offers you to become aware of your dependencies. Welcome any such opportunity, even if it is painful. You will have many of them. They appear every minute. Every minute life offers you an opportunity to become aware of your dependencies. Life is the greatest and the wisest teacher you have. It gives you everything you need to become happy. You just need to see it.

You can say, "What kind of happiness is Pint talking about when I meet awful people day after day? What kind of happiness is he talking about when I am sick every other day? What kind of happiness is he talking about when I don't have the money to pay rent?" I keep saying that life gives you exactly what you need. Your dependencies prevent you from experiencing happiness, and they will only leave you when you see them. In order to see your dependencies, you need to experience the situations you are currently experiencing. These are the lessons you have not passed. The electricity at your house was turned off, and you are screaming your head off. Money was stolen from you, and you are screaming your head off. These situations are given to you so that you can understand your dependency on money.

Life is a constant movement. Something comes, and something goes all the time. That is the beauty of life. Life offers constant change. But we try to stop it. A human being wants to hold on to pleasure, power, and security. In doing that, he kills life. He kills himself. Life provides us with the lessons we need, and they come in different forms. The lesson might come in the form of a new human being or a situation at work. If you are ready to learn, you will accept these lessons, not with an unhappy face but with a curious smile.

Start to work on your dependencies. Let us say you see someone who irritates you. What would you do before? You would get irritated. What are you going to do now? Now, when you feel irritation, you get a curious expression on your face. You say to yourself, "Here is my dependency. Here comes another teacher. I have to sort out the dependency he dramatizes in me." This is the real creativity. You do not have time to be afraid. You are creating. You receive your lessons, and you become aware of them. In this case, they do not recur. Everything is in your hands now. When you start to see and understand dependencies that stand behind your irritation, they leave you. Suddenly, the human being who used to irritate you for many years stops irritating you. Your life starts to change. For example, you come to a place where you used to feel bad, and you find yourself feeling good there. It means one of your dependencies has left you. It is the same place, and the people there are the same, but for some reason you feel good there. This is the indicator that points to the fact that you finally saw one of your dependencies. Your life suddenly becomes very interesting. What do people usually do? They usually run toward things that attract them or away from things that repel them. They live in this constant state of hurry and fear. Is this living?

You do not need to run from anything and anyone anymore. You just need to observe your manifestations in different situations. You cannot run away from yourself anyway. Life will come to you and bring you the lessons you need even if you were to lock yourself in the bathroom for ten years. You will have to learn your lessons. You cannot get away from life. You can continue to hide and not to see. However, this is not a very smart way to learn your lessons. On the other hand, you can accept everything that happens to you as an opportunity to understand yourself in a new way, which is much smarter.

The main law of life is constant movement and change. Life is a river that flows and changes constantly. No one can hold, stop, or appropriate it. Richard Bah illustrates this very well in one of his stories.

Certain creatures live on the bottom of a big, beautiful river. Its flow is rapid and constant. What do these creatures do? They keep grabbing for the seaweed. They think that if they were to stop doing that they would be taken away by the current. All of them are afraid of that, but suddenly, one of them decides to release his hold on the seaweed. No one has done it before. His neighbors scream at him, "Are you nuts? You are going to be crushed against the rocks." He releases his hold anyway. He is thrown against the rocks couple of times and gets bruised a bit, but finally the current takes him to the surface. His neighbors, who still hold on to the seaweed, see him swimming above them and start to talk about him. They call him God. He tells them, "You can do the same. I used to hold onto seaweed tight, but I released my hold. You can do it." They scream, "No. You are great. You can do it. You are God and we are not." He replies, "I am the same creature as you. The only difference between us—I released what I was holding. You have to release what you are holding to so tightly." "No," — they say — "We can't do that. Only you can do that."

Awareness—the road to freedom

When a human being releases everything he used to hold on to in his life, he ascends and becomes a demigod. He becomes who he really is. We all have this option, but most of us do not know about it or are afraid to use it. What do we do all the time? We hold on to something we think is ours. We are afraid to surrender to the current of life. As a result, we live the way we live, i.e. in fear and suffering.

Look at the way most people live. What is the essence of their life? They want to have a house, a car, and a spouse. They do everything they can to get and to hold onto what, as it appears to them, they want. Were they happy getting there? No. They used to say to themselves, "I will be happy when I have a house and a man by my side." They lived with certain expectations. Then they received what they expected. Are they happy now? No. Why? They are not happy because now that they have received what they desired, they are afraid to lose it. So, what do they do now? They frantically hold on to what they have. All their efforts and energy are spent holding onto it and chasing away other women who approach their husbands, chasing away thieves from their cars, and protecting their money in the banks. They do not live; they survive. They are totally occupied and spend all their energy trying to protect what they have. They cannot see that this is impossible. There is nothing stable in this life. Everything around us changes all the time. This is the basic law of life—life changes. Yet, what do people want? They want life to stop. So, what can we do to live a full life? First, we need to become aware of the fact that we are stuck in the prison of our dependencies. Until we realize that we are imprisoned by our dependencies, we will not develop the longing to escape to freedom. If you don't see that you are stuck in life and the same song has been playing for years, you will not want to go anywhere else or listen to another song. If you think that the only thing that makes you happy is chicken soup, you will not try anything else. You will say, "Why? I have my chicken soup. I don't need anything else. My grandfather used to eat this soup. My father used to eat this soup. I ate it all my life, and my kids will eat it too."

Why does it happen this way? We absorb our parents' stereotypes and modes of behavior. We might not like them initially. We can even resist and experience so-called "father—son" conflicts. We say, "No, I will grow up to be different." However, with years passing by, we turn into carbon copies of our parents and teach our kids to do the same.

To receive something new and beautiful that is waiting for us, we need to let go of what we got used to. To put on a new dress, we first need to take off the old one. The main difficulty lies in understanding what I just said. Someone says, "This is very interesting. I want to get to know life." However, when he gets back home, the old pattern repeats itself. Everything is the same again, and he says, "There are people in this world who can be happy, but not me. I have what I have, and I am not going to let go of it."

How do you relate to what we are discussing here? You can experience pleasant feelings now, but then, on your return home to your habitual life, you may forget everything. Why do we have to get together regularly? We must do that because aside from the desire to change ourselves and to understand how to change, we also need to maintain the impulse of self-awareness. Together we can get to places, which is very difficult for a lone seeker to reach. We are not just learning new things together; we support each other. Perhaps this week was very difficult for you. Perhaps you have seen your chief dependency. Your friends will understand and support you. Later on, you will become stronger and you will be able to support others.

CHAPTER 2
ACHIEVING CALMNESS —
"TO BE HERE AND NOW"

• ◆ • ◆ • ◆ • ◆ • ◆ • ◆ • ◆ • ◆ • ◆ • ◆ • ◆ • ◆ • ◆ • ◆ • ◆ • ◆ • ◆ • ◆ •

And an astronomer said, Master, what of Time?
And the Prophet answered:

You would measure time the measureless and the immeasurable. You would adjust your conduct and even direct the course of your spirit according to hours and seasons. Of time you would make a stream upon whose bank you would sit and watch its flowing.

Yet the timeless in you is aware of life's timelessness, and knows that yesterday is but today's memory and tomorrow is today's dream. And that which sings and contemplates in you is still dwelling within the bounds of that first moment which scattered the stars into space.

Who among you does not feel that his power to love is boundless? And yet who does not feel that very love, though boundless, encompassed within the center of his being, and moving not from love thought to love thought, nor from love deeds to other love deeds? And is not time even as love is, undivided and spaceless?

But in your thought you must measure time into seasons, let each season encircle all the other seasons. And let today embrace the past with remembrance and the future with longing.

—Khalil Gibran, *The Prophet, On Time*

How happiness comes

— What does it mean to live here and now? Recall a situation when you were happy, even if for a second. Have you experienced such a state of happiness in your life?

— *Many times.*

— Did you think about the things you had experienced before or about something that expects you in the future during these happy moments?

—*In my greatest moments of happiness I did not think about anything. I was in a very interesting state.*

— This state is called *here and now*. When we are in *here and now*, we feel the calmness and splendor of what is going on around us. The periods of ecstasy and happiness are the moments we are in *here and now*. This is simple. To be happy, you need to be *here and now*. What do we do instead? If we are not *here and now*, where are we?

— *We either think of what we are going to do, or we think about something we did before.*

— Yes. We think about the past or we look toward the future. For example, you are sitting here thinking, "Have I locked the house? What is my kid doing now?" And you are not here anymore; you are by the door of your house or running in the streets looking for your kid. What do people frequently think about? They recall their problems and fears and project them into the future saying, "That's how it is always going to be." Can you be *"here and now"* if you think that way? Can you be happy? No. That is what most people do. If you were to say to such a guy that he already has everything he needs to be happy, he will say, "Are you crazy? What kind of happiness are you talking about? I was almost fired from work yesterday. They can fire me tomorrow. A few days ago, some rough people told me they would beat me up. They can do it at any time." That is what people think about all the time. That is how they make themselves miserable. They live in the past that died already or in the future that has not been born yet. Happiness is a state where you are aware of yourself here and now. The river of life flows here and now, and if we happen to be in the river, we experience the happiness of its movement and it is endless beauty. But to feel such a state we need to submerge ourselves in the river of life and to flow with it. What do we do instead? We try to swim against the current of life. We spend all our energy fighting the current of life, and we get washed ashore. Or we try to swim fast to get ahead of the current, which similarly leads us ashore. But if we were to relax and give ourselves to the current of life, we would feel and enjoy it. For example, you want to talk to a man who is walking. If you were to walk slower than he does, you would not be able to talk to him. If you were to walk faster than him, you would not be able to talk to him either. The only way for you to communicate with him is to walk as fast as he does. If you run ahead of life, you do not feel it. If you drag your feet behind it, you do not feel it either.

The sensation of life is what makes us happy. Only two things stand in our way: thoughts about the past that has ended already, and fantasies about the future that is not here yet. In reality, we have everything we need to be happy; we just need to refuse these excursions in time.

There is another catch here. We can only be *here and now* when we emotionally accept everything that happens around us. For example, you are planning to go on a hike with a friend. You come to the place where you agreed to meet, and you do not find him there. What do you do? You get irritated. You have not accepted the situation. Are you *here and now*? No.

You try to remember, "Did we specify this spot? Did we confirm this time?" You start to question, "Why didn't he show up?" You start to imagine the hike as ruined, and you get upset with him. Suddenly, he shows up.

A flat tire—an Armageddon

Why can't we accept what happens to us? The truth is we must pay for all our dependencies. For example, you feel very good when someone you love is next to you, but when he or she is not around, you feel bad. Can you really accept everything that happens to you emotionally? Can you accept everything life gives you? For example, you are driving a car. Suddenly, you get a flat tire. You jump out of the car screaming, "What's going on?! Why me?! My weekend is ruined again!" You were driving to a picnic expecting to relax, but now, instead of being happily *here and now*, you have this problem. Stop for a minute. Write down what is difficult for you to accept emotionally: your family demands, bus being late, runny nose, or a salary cut?

— That's how we make ourselves unhappy. That's how we create and maintain our negative emotions. How can a man be calm here? When you start to accept everything life gives you, you start to experience calmness. The only reason we are not calm and happy is that we are not *here and now*. We don't allow ourselves to experience this inner calmness. Life provides us with an opportunity to be *here and now*, but we say, "No, it is bad *here and now*. We want to be over there." We start to think how good we felt the day before yesterday, and how good it would be for that state to repeat itself tomorrow. Some of us experience one happy moment and then spend our entire life reminiscing about it. They meet someone they like and spend all their life concentrating on him or her. This someone left them long time ago or died, but they are still thinking about him.

The old Buddhist parable illustrates this point well. A monk was walking through a forest. Suddenly, he saw a tiger running at him. He turned around and started to run. He ran for a long time and found himself on top of a cliff. He started to descend, lost his footing, and started to fall. As he fell, he grabbed a tree branch that broke his fall. He looked down and saw another tiger walking along the bottom of the precipice. He looked up and saw the first tiger eyeing him from above. As he contemplated the situation, he saw a strawberry growing next to him and he heard the tree break under his weight. What did he do? He grabbed the strawberry and devoured it with pleasure. That is what it means to live *here and now*. However, most people prefer to live afraid of tigers, not tasting strawberries.

They say that a coward dies a thousand times while a courageous man only dies once. It is easy to make yourself miserable. How do you do it?

— *A man can live in the past, thinking about the mistakes he has made and brooding over his inability to correct them, or he can come to terms with these mistakes. He can also live in the future.*

— I will tell you how you can make yourself miserable at home. You should frequently think in this manner: "I have married you, and you ruined ten years of my life. And you keep ruining it." Instead, you look at your spouse and think, "You got me upset yesterday, and you are going to do the same thing tomorrow."

On the other hand, you can also think about how good you feel together. In this case, you will not make yourself unhappy. You have a choice: you can make yourself happy or unhappy.

30

The amount of energy you spend on these choices is the same. Which do you prefer? How much time do you spend in these states? **To be *here and now* is to be completely aware of your thoughts, feelings, and actions.** However, most people do not even know what it means to feel. Can they feel happiness? Happiness is an experience, not a thought. To feel happiness, you need to open up to it, to allow yourself to feel. Many people are afraid to feel, because when they start to feel they may feel pain or something they consider to be bad. The first step is to allow yourself to feel everything. Otherwise, you are not going to feel happiness—not because you are unable to feel it, but because you did not allow yourself to feel it. Become aware of yourself, of your thoughts, feelings, and actions.

— *If you ask me what I did two hours ago, I would probably recall that, but what I thought and felt two hours ago ... I doubt I will be able to recall that.*

Ask a thief why he steals

— My friend shared a story with me a few days ago. A passerby approached him on the street and asked for a cigarette. When he said that he did not have one, the man hit him hard. My friend took it to the police. The police found his offender and asked him, "Do you know what you have done?" His reply was, "No. What did I do?" — "You hit a man this morning, and he is pressing charges against you." "You got it all wrong," the man said, "I asked this bastard for a cigarette, and he did not give me one."

Many people are unaware of what they do. They blame everyone around instead. Whom do you blame?

For example, you say, "I wanted to go to the movies. You have prevented me from doing that. You started this argument, and now, instead of enjoying the movie, I have to sit here and argue with you." That is what people do all the time. When we feel bad, we start to blame others for it. If your mind is occupied with how bad things are and how dangerous the world is, you will not be calm. Where did you get these thoughts? Are they yours? Ask your friend, "Is this what you're thinking?" He will answer, "No." Ask a thief why he steals. He will answer that it is impossible not to steal. Ask a killer why he kills, and he will say, "It is impossible not to kill. Everything is made in such a way here that I have to kill. The world forces me to do that." Ask a man who cries, and he will answer, "The world forces me to cry. Someone just hit me. My wife has left me for my friend. I was robbed yesterday. How can I not cry?" He thinks that the world influences him. He thinks he is the result of this influence. He thinks he cannot change anything. This is the difference between a man who is aware of himself and one who is not.

People commit crimes because they are not aware of themselves. When asked, "Why did you do that?" they say, "Everything around me forced me to do that." They don't understand what they do. They are not aware of what they do. A man comes to work coughing. He is told, "Please, go home. You are sick. You will infect everyone here." But no one sends people home to get better from the disease called "not aware of myself." They continue to scream and argue. Isn't this the most dangerous infection? They spread panic and depression with their words. Are they ever stopped? No. We consider it normal.

— *What if it is my boss? I cannot say anything to my boss.*

— If you think you can't say anything, you will not say anything. Actually, a boss represents his employees. If you think you cannot say anything to your boss, you will get a boss that you will not be able to say anything to.

Do you want to know your main problem?

— There is another interesting detail here. It deals with what irritates us the most in other people. What do you usually blame other people for? Do you blame people for not understanding you? Do you blame people for not doing what they need to do?

Do you want to know your main problem? Buy yourself a mirror, and when you want to accuse someone, take a look in it. You will see your face there, and it will tell you something very important. These words and the expression of that face are directed not toward someone else, but toward you. Take a look, and you will see everything. That everything is the most important thing for you.

Perhaps, this face will scream, "Be nicer to me. Understand me. Hear me out. Why are you always like that?" Everything you are going to see and hear is related to you. You speak to yourself, but you do not know that.

Life is a mirror. People are mirrors. If you really want to understand and to become aware of what is happening to you, i.e. of what you think, feel, and do—this mirror will help you.

People as mirrors will reflect your feelings. When you scream at someone, be aware that you are screaming at yourself and about yourself. If you do that, you will understand everything. You will understand that you are not screaming at someone else, you are screaming at yourself. In reality, everything we say, we say to ourselves, not to other people. We try, but we cannot hear ourselves, that's why we scream so loudly.

After having the same conversation for fifteen years, you suddenly heard yourself. That's illumination. Please, record what you have said on your cell phone and listen to what you were trying to say to yourself for years. Perhaps, you will finally understand that you were talking to yourself but were unable to hear it.

Everything you say, at the level of consciousness where you happen to be at the moment, activate the same words and the same level of consciousness in another human being. As a result, he starts to "vibrate" at your level of vibration.

For example, it is very easy to start a fight. You just have to approach someone and tell him that he is an idiot. If that's not enough for him, add a profanity, and you will reach your goal. Do you understand what happens when you insult another human being?

No, you don't. You act surprised and say, "What is this? I came with the best intentions. I told him that his socks stink. This is the truth. To another man I said, "This tie does not look good on you." And this is the truth. Do you want to be truthful or to be happy? Think about it.

The higher the level of consciousness we occupy, the fewer disagreements develop between us. The higher the level of consciousness we occupy, the less we want to accuse others and the more we feel that all of us are one.

Suddenly you start to feel that every one of us is very important and that a human being you have screamed at all your life is very important to you because he is your mirror. He was performing the difficult work of constantly "mirroring" you.

And what if he was not there? You would have never learned how rough and insulting to others you were, not ever feeling it. You would have never found how callous you were without his unwilling help. It is he who constantly reminds you of it. You just don't want to see it in yourself. Once you start to see, you will see the important role this human being has played in your life.

— *Does another human being "mirror" his own states through us too?*

— Of course he "mirrors." But that is a different question. Let us get to know ourselves first and then teach others. We all want to teach others. The wisdom of this world is that whatever one man says to another is important for both of them.

Everything is made so well here that one has to be a total idiot not to learn.

You say something and what you say is related to you and to the man you are saying it to. Both of you can find it useful. But when people learn the law of "mirroring", they start to say to people that are close to them, "Everything you say is related to you. It has to do with you. Here is a book, read it, it's there. So, remember what you just said. Think about it, and remember that I told you that."

Wise people try to hear themselves and to become aware of what they say. They attempt to become aware of the truth in themselves. If something touched or irritated you, it is important precisely for you.

How do we create our world? If hatred is inside us, what kind of a world is going to be outside of us? It is going to be full of hate. If fear is inside us, what kind of a world is going to be outside of us? It is going to be full of fear. And if happiness is inside us, what kind of a world is it going to be? It is going to be a happy world. So, what does our perception of the world depend on? It depends on our state. And our state depends on us.

If you have not understood this by now, it is because you are not aware of yourself. A man who is aware of himself understands that he creates his own world. You create your internal and external world yourself. If happiness is inside you, everything around you is happy. If horror is inside yo, then only horror, suffering, and hate is outside.

Everything you see around you represents your inner projection. The people next to you reflect what you have inside you. An enlightened human being is a human being who sees the wisdom and happiness of the world. Whatever happens around him, he is calm and happy. He may appear crazy to other people, but in reality, he is the only normal person here. Others are crazy, because they see partially. He sees holistically. He creates his world himself. You don't need to change the world to be happy; you need to change your perception. To do that, you need to be constantly aware of what you feel, think, and do. Otherwise, you will always be occupied with other people and your surroundings, not understanding that you create your world yourself. A man who is not aware of himself tries to manipulate the world in order to adjust it to his dependencies. This is madness. No one can do that.

The disinclination to see yourself gives birth to fear

Stalin tried to adjust the world to his fears. He died in fear. He was constantly afraid. Why did so many people die during his reign? He was afraid to be killed. He was afraid that something he didn't want to happen would happen. What did he achieve by submitting the entire country to his dependencies? The only thing he achieved was to die in fear. That's what every dictator achieves. Not a single tyrant has ever achieved what he wanted to achieve. Hitler went crazy at the end of his life. That's how they all end up, because what they want to achieve is impossible.

The only true way is to look inside. You can't look at what other people do, appraising what they do to be right or wrong; you can only look inside. Otherwise, you are going to spend your life blaming them. Only the aware human being can accept himself fully and wholly, with all his thoughts, feelings, and actions. Why is a man afraid to look at himself and to become aware of what he thinks, feels, and does? He is afraid to do that because he believes he will see something bad in himself. For example, you have observed your desire to kill someone. You allowed yourself to feel it, and you are shocked. "How can this be? How could I feel that way? How can a nice guy like me want to kill anyone? No, this is not my thought."

Suddenly, you feel you want to do something that is not condoned by the society in which you are living. You get scared and you say, "No, this is not what I feel. I can't do that. I am good. This can't be me." That's why many people are so afraid to look inside themselves. They are afraid to see what they don't want to see in themselves.

Every human being contains everything humanity contains. You may feel everything: a desire to kill, a desire to rob, and a desire to rape. If you allow yourself to look inside yourself, you will see everything there. You don't need to close yourself inside a monastery to become aware of yourself. No, the best place for you to become aware of yourself is where you are now: at home with your family, at work with your coworkers, in the middle of a city surrounded by your countrymen, and during the time in which you live. You are provided with every condition necessary for you to solve your assignments. You can only solve them by becoming aware of your thoughts, feelings, and actions. What is meditation? It's awareness. You are doing something, and you become aware of it. When you start to become aware of yourself, i.e. to observe the thoughts and emotional states you are in, you start to see that those are not your thoughts. You feel a desire to kill, but this is not you who wants to kill. These are not your thoughts. Do you give birth to these thoughts? No. They simply pass through your brain as clouds pass through the skies. A great number of thoughts pass through your brain.

You have been to many places where people gather, and you may have felt how the atmospheres of these places differ. If you have been to the places where criminals gather, you have probably felt fear and anxiety there. These people attract the thoughts and emotional states connected to fear. They are afraid, and the atmosphere of the places in which they gather is saturated with fear. You have caught these emanations, but in reality, they have nothing to do with you. They attract these thoughts from every side. Every human being is surrounded by an aura that consists of different thoughts and feelings. Our auras are made of the thoughts we constantly feed and maintain. When you think these thoughts frequently, i.e. when you recreate and repeat them, they solidify. Some of these thoughts become so strong that they realize themselves in your life. These thoughts determine your fate, because when you think about something frequently, you create it on the physical plane. The thoughts you cultivate and hold on to are very important. But different thoughts may pass through your mind. For example, a thought such as, "Why don't I hit this man?" can pass through your mind. Or you may observe yourself thinking, "I don't love my mother! Do I really think that? Do I hate my father?! It can't be. This is madness." You get scared. Why are you scared? **Until you can impartially observe any thought that passes through your mind, you will not be able to free yourself from fear.** Do you understand what I am saying? Actually, you need to receive your own experience of self-observation. Just to talk about it is not enough.

Awareness solves every problem

I constantly observe what happens to me. I become aware of it. When I wake up in the morning, I become aware of my body, and I scan it with my inner attention. I observe its every sensation. I feel and become aware of every part of it. I become aware of the feelings present in it. I become aware of my thoughts. I try to be simultaneously aware of everything I think, feel, sense, say, and do. This is what it means to be fully aware. When you start to practice this yourself, you will find that it might be easier for you to be aware of what's going on in your body. For example, how you walk or physically do something. You may find that it is difficult for you to observe

39

your feelings. For example, you may find it difficult to become aware of the moment when you start to feel bad. You may find it difficult to observe how this feeling develops. Every state, as with a car accident, starts at a certain moment in time. Every disease also starts at a certain moment in time. If you become aware of it in the very beginning, it is easier to get rid of it. If you miss this early phase, it is much more difficult to do so. The same can be said about any emotional state. You catch a certain feeling, a feeling of fear for example, the same way you catch a cold. When you are not aware of yourself, you don't understand what is going on with you. You catch the feeling and sensation of fear and you proceed to carry it. You are not aware of it. You may notice this fear a few hours later, when it will get stronger and mandate that you pay attention to it. Three hours have passed. The feeling of fear has become amplified in you during that time. You start to feel it only when it becomes very strong. You could have felt it in the beginning. You could have noticed it the moment it came to you. This is only possible if you were aware of yourself at the time. You can pass multiple thoughts and feelings through you. You don't need to hold on to them. You don't need to accumulate them.

You may have some knowledge about the topic we are discussing, but this is not enough. To know about it is not enough. You need to do it all the time. You need to be aware of yourself in different situations. In that case, you may notice that during the last two hours you were totally unaware of yourself. But you can only understand that if you constantly remember your intention to observe and to be aware of yourself. You will see that you are happy only during those periods of your life when you are fully aware of yourself. During these moments, you feel that there is nothing to fear in the world, because as you become aware of something you are afraid of, it disappears. You need to try different methods of self-observation. You need to constantly experiment with them. We are all different; what works for one of us may not work for another. What is dependency? It is unawareness. If you really want to become aware of yourself, you will use every negative emotion for this purpose. As a result, you will become a more aware human being. When you start to observe and become aware of yourself, you will see many things that you did not accept in other people, and as a result, you did not see them in yourself. When you reach this moment, you may start to dislike yourself. You may say, "No, this is not me." If you do that, your growth will stop. Everything you experience with all your so-called weaknesses is you, i.e. this is the very best you have at this stage of your development. What would you do if you were a perfect human being? We are here to understand and to become aware of who we are and to change something in ourselves. But in order to change ourselves we need to understand where we are now. Yes, you feel anger. When you see someone, you want to scream at him and hit him. Yes, this is who you are now. This is your current best and this is beautiful. We are all on the way to our wholeness. Our deficiencies represent the important steps on this evolutionary ladder. We step on them in order to climb higher. Without them there would not be any development. To walk this way, we must accept ourselves completely, with all our shortcomings. What you previously could not accept in yourself, you will become aware of and accept now.

What does it mean to accept yourself *here and now*, and what is *here and now*? All your thoughts, emotions, and actions create your "**here and now**." You need to see and to become aware of them. Many people cannot accept certain desires which they harbor. For example, you cannot accept your desire to smoke. You need to decide whether you want to continue to smoke or not, and either quit or continue to smoke, but you should not make a problem out of it. Some of you eat a lot. Stop overeating or continue to overeat, but if you continue to do it, do it with pleasure. Accept who you are. When you do that, something will change, and perhaps you will stop eating so much. Allow yourself to do what you have been forbidding yourself to do. Quite frequently, this permission on your part will lead to the problem disappearing on its own. Many things occur only because you don't accept them. For example, a child is screaming, and no one understands what he needs. As you approach him, he smiles and stops screaming. He just wanted someone to look at him. The same thing happens inside of you. Someone screams there, "Look at me! Look at me!" but you say, "No." You don't accept yourself, so your inner parts continue to scream. They do what they do because they want to have some of your attention. They are inside of you. You need to become aware of them. All of humanity is inside each one of us. Every previous generation is inside us. We have all played different roles in the history of humanity. And we know these roles very well. So, why do you get upset when you see something so-called horrible? This is our history. A killer kills because he is not aware; he does not understand what he is doing. If a human being kills another human being, he is crazy. Whether psychiatrists accept him as crazy or not is irrelevant—he is crazy. Would a human being who is aware of himself kill another human being? The one who is aware of himself understands that everything he does will return to him.

Once upon a time, a thief came to a teacher. "I am a thief," he told him. — "I know." — "I want to stop doing what I do, but I can't. I decided to steal a very precious necklace from the

42

shah's palace tonight." — "Do it, but be aware of every step you take and everything you do. Be aware of everything when you start on your journey tonight. Be aware of your every feeling and your every thought tonight." The thief said, "I will do what you ask me to do." At dawn, he came to the teacher and said, "You are a sly old man. I was unable to steal. I am the best thief of Baghdad, yet I was unable to steal last night. When I started to observe myself, I had to stop."

You are both an actor and a spectator at the same time

A human being is an actor. A human being is an actor in the show of his own life who got overexcited with the roles he plays and forgot who he really is. A true actor lives in two worlds at the same time. He lives as a spectator and as the character he plays. He observes what he does. He plays a role, and he observes how he plays it.

Most people are completely identified with the roles they play. They are not aware of themselves as actors. In their own lives, they lose the sensation that we have all felt while watching a good movie. Have you seen *King Lear*? If you were in the shoes of the king, abandoned by everyone, you would feel really bad. But while sitting in front of your TV, you experience esthetic pleasure from watching the show. You can relate to the roles you play in your life in the same way.

Have you ever thought about this? Your Real "I" observes every role you play. Be your Real "I". If you consider yourself to be just the body-mind, and this body-mind experiences hatred, you can't do anything but to experience it in full. But if you know that all of this is a show, that you are not a body, not a feeling, and not a thought, but are something that observes it all, everything changes. Can you become aware of your thoughts? **Have you become aware of one of your thoughts today?** You are more than your thoughts. If you were a thought, could you have become aware of it? No. **Have you become aware of one of your feelings today?** Have you become aware of the feeling of fear, love, or hate? If yes, you are more than your feelings. **Have you become aware of one of the sensations of your body today?** If yes, you are more than your body. You are more than your body, thoughts, and feelings combined. You are pure consciousness.

Can you imagine your own funeral? How can you do that if you are only a body that is slowly dying? So, you are more than just a body that is slowly dying. You are more than anything you consider yourself to be. You are more than all your problems. Does this knowledge make you happy? This knowledge will allow you to see your life from the side and to experience the pleasure of life. Your body has dependencies, but your spirit does not. Spirit is the energy of true love. It is a state of eternity, lightness, and total freedom. There is no me. There is something enormous, beautiful, and unknown. Our language lacks the words to describe this feeling. This is a state of eternity. But many people, even when they have experienced this state, turn on their minds and start to appraise the situation. They ask, "What is it? How is that possible? What is it for? How can I prolong this state?" They try to define this feeling by using words. You can't do that. You need to live in this state. You must simply live in it. You don't need to understand anything. You just need to live it.

CHAPTER 3
DIFFERENT PLANES OF COMMUNICATION

You were born together, and together you shall be forevermore.
You shall be together when the white wings of death scatter your days.
Ay, you shall be together even in the silent memory of God.
But let there be spaces in your togetherness,
And let the winds of the heavens dance between you.

Love one another, but make not a bond of love:
Let it rather be a moving sea between the shores of your souls.
Fill each other's cup but drink not from one cup.
Give one another of your bread but eat not from the same loaf
Sing and dance together and be joyous, but let each one of you be alone,
Even as the strings of a lute are alone though they quiver with the same music.

Give your hearts, but not into each other's keeping.
For only the hand of Life can contain your hearts.
And stand together yet not too near together:
For the pillars of the temple stand apart,
And the oak tree and the cypress grow not in each other's shadow.

—Kahlil Gibran, *The Prophet, On Marriage*

Upon what are relationships built?

— On what do we build our relationships with other people?

— *Relationships between people are built upon certain ethical norms.*

— *Relationships between people are built on their needs and the satisfaction of these needs.*

— But why do we have to build these relationships with other people? Why do we need to communicate with other people? Some people don't like to talk to other people. A famous ancient philosopher lived in a barrel and did not talk to people at all. He could understand quite a bit based solely on this experience.

Why do we interact with people? Why do we get in contact with people if these painful states of irritation, jealousy, hatred, and fear appear as the result of our interactions with them? Perhaps one should not interact with people. Perhaps one should never get married…

— *People build their relationships based on common interests and their desire to get to know each other. People want to get to know the world, and they do that through their relationships with other people.*

— Are you satisfied with the relationships you have, or do you want to change them?

— *I am interested in getting to know new people.*

— What do you expect from these new acquaintances?

— *I want to get to know my new sides through them.*

— What do you want from these new people? Are you looking for a friend, a lover, or a spouse? We all have certain notions about how our friends, lovers, wives, or husbands should be.

— *Yes, I have a certain ideal image, and I look for someone to fit this ideal image.*

— Exactly. A woman looks for an ideal husband and finds an average man. She tries to make the ideal husband out of him, but he does not fit the picture that she has in her mind. That leads to arguments, fights, and eventually it ends in a divorce. It seems to me that people don't communicate with each other but with their ideals, i.e. they want to see other people the way they want to see them, not the way they really are. And what do they experience because of this?

— *They experience discomfort.*

— What do you experience when a certain human being does not correspond to your expectations? What do you feel when he does not do what you want him to do?

— *I feel irritated.*

— How do you feel when your relationship with your man brings you pain and disenchantment?

— *In a situation like this, I usually see that the ideal image I painted does not fit the human being with whom I am dealing.*

— Why do these relationships lead to suffering? What is the reason for these sufferings, you or another human being?

— *The reason is in me. I have created a certain image, and I was looking for a human being to fit this image, instead of seeing a real human being.*

— Does the image created by you prevail in your relationships? How often do you try to fit a human being into what you want instead of trying to see and to accept what he really is? How often do you see a human being the way he really is, not the way you want him to be?

— *Sometimes I even forget there is a live human being with his own interests in front of me. In forgetting that, I start to pursue my own aims. Sometimes I have a very difficult time switching out of that mode, but with certain people, I snap out of it fast. Once I start to listen to another human being, I see how our relationship changes. It is very exciting to see how his attitude toward me changes. He might even look differently when he starts to talk about things that interest him.*

— Many people try to manipulate others, i.e. they try to fit them to what they want to see. They are not interested in what these people want; rather, they try to fit them to something they want. For example, you want a certain man to be with you. You may feel scared or deprived of something when he is not around. You want him to be with you all the time. Have you experienced a state like this?

— *I have experienced this state quite a few times. A human being who manipulates others is looking for his own profit. He only thinks about himself, and he does everything for himself. He never thinks about his partner. As a result, he does not reach what he wants and can't build real relationships; it's a mutual manipulation.*

I tried to make what I want out of him, but ...

— Holistic relationships presuppose taking into account the interests of both sides. When one side tries to conduct its interests and policies, the second side becomes passive. I have seen many such cases. A woman consulted me a few days ago. She was not satisfied with the relationship she had with her husband. She said she knew exactly what kind of a husband she needed. She described her ideal partner in minute details. I asked her whether the man she was currently with satisfied all her requirements. "No, not all of them," she answered. "I've tried to make what I want out of him for the last fifteen years, but I was not successful." I asked her whether she was happy now. "No," she said, "I feel horrible now. I made a floor mop out of him." Imagine that. She spent fifteen years trying to make something out of a human being, and now she feels horrible. And the human being she has married does not exist anymore. She made something else out of him. She broke him to pieces, and she is not interested in him anymore. That's how manipulation can end, when you only consider your own interests.

— *That happens quite frequently. I feel regret afterwards, but …*

— You say, "I want only good things for us. You just don't understand. Why don't you stay home with me tonight?" And he refuses one of his interests. Then he refuses another interest, and then another interest. Eventually, he loses all his interests. Are you interested in a man who has no interests? A human being who has no interests has no energy. These people usually get sick. That's what this can lead to. I review extreme situations when you force someone to do something he does not like to do, or don't allow him to do what he likes to do. People get energy when they do something they are interested in, and if all the opportunities to do what they are interested in are cut off, they lose energy. He will sit next to you, and he will not do anything he wants to do or do something he does not want to do. As a result, he starts to lose energy. Then he gets sick. The disease progresses, becomes chronic, and pretty soon you have a sick, boring guy next to you.

— *A dead man who is still alive.*

— Yes, he is barely alive. He is not dead yet. He survives somehow. You need to take care of him. You turn into his nurse, because he does not want anything anymore. He has almost no energy. You wanted him to be with you? He is with you. He is sick in bed all the time. Now you are dependent on him, because you have to take care of him. I am reviewing this extreme case, but this is how the manipulation of another human being frequently ends.

— We have reviewed the relationship between a husband and a wife, but human communication involves other spheres. I brought ethics up because the ethics of relationships determines the relationship between people in general. When people get to know each other, the questions of upbringing and ethical norms start to operate right away. A human being can adjust his behavior according to the rules society imposes on him, which may result in him not behaving the way he wants to behave. Everything gets twisted here.

— Can you force another human being to do what he does not want to do?

— Yes, this is called oppression.

— But in this case, people who do what they don't want to do allow themselves to be oppressed. They give other people permission to oppress them.

— What about a "broken will"? A man did what he wanted to do, but someone came and broke him. I've finished reading a book about Erdman yesterday. He was a great writer. They broke him and sent him to a concentration camp.

— Do you see yourself in this writer?

— No.

— No? Then why do you talk about him? You want to convince me that a man can be broken, but I say that a man can withstand any conditions.

— Not everyone. It depends on one's upbringing and energy supply.

Oppressed by society

— Can you clarify what you want to say? You brought up a particular example which underlines a certain tendency that you consider to be true. What exactly do you want to say?

— I want to say that society imposes strict rules on communication which do not allow people to communicate the way they want to

communicate. I think civilization imposes a certain imprint on communication, and this imprint is negative.

— Does anyone else want to say something?

— *I agree with the statement that civilization imposes a certain imprint on communication, but I think this imprint changes when we start to become aware of ourselves. When a man starts to become aware of himself, society's influence on him diminishes.*

— It is possible to force something onto a human being only if he does not know himself, i.e. when he accepts societal norms as his own norms. In such a state, he cannot separate himself from the multiple rules and regulations that exist in society, organizations, corporations, etc. A man who cannot do that is doomed to suffer. Take a look and you will see that these rules, regulations, norms, and laws which come out of the notion "ought to" are very controversial; quite frequently, they contradict each other. A man who thinks that he needs to comply with all of them may go crazy, as quite frequently these laws and norms don't reflect the true nature of the relationship between people.

— *We live in a highly oppressed society. We were oppressed for a long time. Do you agree with that?*

— Do you like it?

— *What do you mean? Do I like the fact that we were oppressed?*

— Do you like the fact that you are living in such a society?

— *We cannot do anything about it.*

— What are you trying to prove now?

— *What can we do? We are all oppressed by the past.*

— You have to stop being oppressed. You must stop allowing everyone to oppress you.

— *Have you ever seen someone who was oppressed for a long time? Have you seen someone whose will was broken?*

— You have asked me what to do, and I told you what to do.

— *Why are you telling me this? I was never oppressed.*

— Then why are you talking about it? **I have asked you to talk only about yourself. Everything I say is based on my own experience, and I want to talk to people who speak about their own experience.**

— *Are you talking about some specific oppression?*

— What do you want to say now? Try to understand what you want to say.

— *What does it mean to be brought up well? I could never understand that. Does it mean that one must suppress one's emotions and be insincere? What does it mean to be natural, and what does it mean to be insincere? I can't understand it.*

— A well-brought up human being is someone who corresponds to the norms of the place where these norms are called *good upbringing*. A well-brought up human being is not necessarily a happy human being.

— *Should we all be brought up well? Should we all be happy with each other?*

— I didn't say that.

— *Should we suppress negative emotions?*

— When a man says he should do something, I always ask: why and for what purpose?

— *For each other. We should make each other happy when we communicate, should not we?*

Make me happy!

— Okay. Try to make me happy.

— *I want to irritate you now. I have a strong desire to irritate you.*

— I understand. You just told me that we should make other people happy, and I am telling you: "Do that! Make me happy!"

— *I irritate you, and this makes you happy.*

— Take a look at how everything can be brought from head to toe when a human being acts not out of his heart desire, but from all these *have to's* and *ought to's* forced on him by the society in which he lives. By following these rules and regulations, you slowly come to understand who you really are. You do things that are required of you which do not satisfy your essence. Thus, you feel bad.

— *This is horrible. Our upbringing starts and ends with "you have to" and "you ought to." You have to be nice and clean. You have to go to school. You have to clean after yourself. You have to keep the fork in your left hand and knife in the right hand. You always have to and ought to do something.*

— Now you understand that these *have to* and *ought to* do not correspond to your true needs.

— *Why am I being forced to do that? Would you be uncomfortable seeing me holding a fork in my right hand?*

— I did not say that.

— *Would you?*

— This is your right. You can hold your knife and fork the way you want.

— *It seems to me that even if you were to put your legs on a table or to hold your fork in the wrong hand, I would not feel uncomfortable if I accept you the way you are. Everything depends on the way we relate to a human being. If I accept someone the way he is, it does not matter to me whether he is using table utensils properly or not. I simply accept and love him.*

— Let's consider this. We are talking about the fact that most people don't know themselves. At the same time, some of them understand that what is being inflicted on them does not correspond to their true wishes. When something is being inflicted on you, and you are told that you have to do it, you don't feel pleasure and enthusiasm doing it. If your action comes out of your essence, the external coercion loses its meaning. It is not necessary. Why should you force someone to do something if he wants to do it himself? Things that are forced on us are perceived as foreign by us. Then the question arises, "What should I do if I am not satisfied with this situation? What should I do if I don't know anything else?"

Some people start to reject what they are forced to do. If the society in which they live says that they need to be acculturated, smile, and be polite, they start to do the opposite. When they are told, "You have to be good," they start to behave badly. When they are told, "You have to be polite," they become rude. But in reality, they are not acting out of their essence here either. They are behaving the way they used to behave, except with the opposite sign now. If previously they subordinated themselves to society's requirements, now they resist these requirements. However, the situation remains the same.

The only way for you to liberate yourself is to go deep inside yourself. You must feel yourself not as a persona or personality, not as a part of something that was inflicted on you, not as a role you play in your family or workplace, but as something that is outside every role, as something that is deep inside you.

— *But a human being who allows himself to be himself will be rejected by society as someone not useful and oppositional.*

— Yes, that's what frequently happens.

— *Is this happiness? Will one be happy if one is himself but alone?*

Society is in you, and you are in society

— If you try to find happiness by following the norms predetermined by society, norms that don't come from the true necessities of a human being, you will not be successful. At best, you will become a normal, adjusted to society personality. This is the goal most psychologists set up for themselves, i.e. to adapt their clients to society. When a client comes to them, they try to understand how he or she *drops out* of society and try to return him back. But the society in which we live is abnormal. One cannot be normal in an abnormal society. We need to understand this. If you want to be yourself instead of being adjusted to society, you will have to deal with something very different. In a societal structure, you have to act as it demands. Sometimes, quite rarely, societal norms may correspond to the true requirements of a human being, but most frequently, we are dealing with the opposite situation.

— *Can one be himself and live in society?*

— I do not encourage you to drop out of society. I urge you to be in society and to be who you are at the same time.

— *But in that case, society will reject us.*

— The society in which we live is very diverse. Certain parts of this society will reject you, but people who are building a new society, a society that will be based on the true necessities of a human being, will not reject you. This new society must be created; it will not be borne by itself. It appears as the result of the aware movement in a new direction. The old always contradicts the new. When you start to become aware of yourself, you start to change. At this point, you stop corresponding to the norms and moral standards that inhibit your understanding of yourself. This is not a discrepancy between you and someone else, but between the new you and the old you. Do you want to be on the side of the new or on the side of the old? Do you want to evolve or degrade? A human being is the only creature on Earth that has the opportunity to understand and to become aware of itself. Animals do not have this opportunity. Born as a cat, a cat will die as a cat. It does not have a choice. It cannot turn into anything else. A human being, on the other hand, can transform into something else. A human being **has this potential**. If he doesn't apply any effort to realize this opportunity, he will degrade. The law of entropy states that whatever you don't work on degrades. If you don't apply any effort to work on self-development and self-awareness, yet at the same time you pacify yourself with the idea that you evolve, you are submerged in an illusion. In reality, you degrade. To evolve, you must apply effort, effort directed to overcoming the old in yourself. A human being who really wants to develop gets to know and understand himself, starts to evolve and enters the opposition with his old self. For development to continue, he needs to constantly be aware of the old in himself, of the old he does not need anymore. Everything old that a society has is also present in every human being. You say you will contradict society. In reality, you are contradicting your old image of yourself, the part of yourself that supports and shares the opinion of the old. We are talking about ourselves, because everything we call society is inside every human being, in his inner world. The world of each one of us has everything in it. When you speak about society, you actually speak about your own parts, which are the continuation of this society. When you speak about your soul, you speak about a certain part of you that expresses something new, beautiful, and limitless; something you can strive for. All of this is in every one of us. The inner world of a human being contains everything. But if we don't see something in ourselves, we can't do anything with it. You say, "I cannot do anything with the society I live in. It is big and powerful; I can't do anything about it."

You can change it. But you can only do that by changing yourself. When you change something in you, it will change everything around you. For example, you cannot externally influence the war in Afghanistan, but you can change your inner part that continues this war.

What takes people to war? Why do they hold guns in their hands? Why do people kill each other? What forces them to do that? Is it anger, jealousy, wrath, or extreme self-love? Don't we all harbor these feelings inside us? Does the presence of these feelings in each and every one of us contribute to the wars we see around us? Every one of us! Don't we have the same feelings and thoughts that prompt some people to reach for arms and kill each other? It is easy to criticize criminals from the comfort of your living room, while sitting in front of the TV saying, "What do they do? What do they create?!" Look inside yourself, and you will see the same feelings there, the same feelings may one day lead you to do what they do.

You ask me what to do? You need to see all these feelings inside yourself.

"I get upset because people upset me..."

— *It is difficult for me to accept the fact that I harbor these feelings. It is very difficult for me to accept that I have these parts.*

— *When one accepts that he has anger and wrath inside, something new opens up, and life becomes much more interesting. I could not allow myself to yell at people before. I did not allow myself to manifest my anger. I allow myself to do that now. Naturally, people reply in a similar fashion. But at the same time, new relationships develop, and they are different from the relationships I had before. This is something new.*

— Until we want to know what is inside us, we cannot know anything new. We cannot understand the world. If we don't acknowledge the presence of anger, jealousy, and hatred in ourselves, we will continue to see the world and ourselves partially and fragmentally, i.e. not holistically. In that case, we project all these feelings onto other people and perceive the world as something incomplete, dangerous, and horrible. That's how we doom ourselves to eternal complaints and dissatisfaction. Why do we do that? We do that, because everything is in us, but we don't want to see it. We need to see that everything is inside us. When you start to see all these feelings and emotions inside yourself, you start to understand that other people look exactly like you. When you see that, you start to develop the seeds of compassion. How can you understand another human being if you consider him to be different from you? How can you understand another human being if you consider him to be a scoundrel? How can you understand another human being if you consider yourself to be higher than him? You can hate him, but you cannot love him. If, on the other hand, you start to see what you don't like in him in yourself and accept it, you start to relate to him with compassion. There is no other way to do it.

There is an old story about an ascetic who sat meditating in a cave. Suddenly, a mouse scurried in and nibbled at his sandal. In annoyance the ascetic opened his eyes.

- Why are you disturbing me in my contemplation?
- I'm hungry, squeaked the mouse.
- Go away, silly mouse. I am seeking oneness with God. How could you think of disturbing me?

- How do you propose to become one with God, asked the mouse, if you can't even become one with me?

— *I have a problem. I have discovered that reactions, such as aggression for example, work automatically. I see them now, but it is very difficult to break the habitual model of interaction with the external world.*

— As you look deeper and deeper inside yourself, you will see many mechanical reactions. They are imposed upon you by societal norms and upbringing. They are not you. They represent a mechanism, a mechanical reaction. "Stimulus—Reaction." Someone stepped on my foot, and I immediately hit him back. Someone insulted me, and I got upset. Someone screamed at me, and I started to scream back. A human being usually acts mechanically, stereotypically. Once you start to investigate yourself deeper and deeper as a mechanism, as a collection of stereotypes, you will see the enormous role that these stereotypes play in your life. Your relationships with people are built on these stereotypes. These stereotypes get downloaded into your ego structure in the process of upbringing and education by parents, teachers, acquaintances, etc. For example, when your mother was upset, she used to tell you that men are scoundrels who should not be trusted. Someone else here was told that women are sly tricksters. You developed a stereotypical perception of relationships with certain people and groups of people. Later on, it becomes self-explanatory and habitual for you. It becomes a mechanism of your nature, your character, your personality. But where is your true self? Is your true self in these stereotypes and mechanical reactions? No, you are not there. You are dealing with a set of rules and recommendations that you have not even proofread. They are based on someone else's experience, and perhaps on the absence of this experience. Moreover, this experience did not bring happiness to people who transferred these recommendations to you. You have started to use it, without even checking whether it works or not. As a result, you repeat the unhappy fate of the person who transmitted them to you. So, unhappy people, parents for example, give birth to other unhappy people—their children. And the army of unhappy people grows exponentially. But we have another option. If only one human being becomes happy, he will start to transmit his understanding of how to be happy to others. Some people will internalize his experience and prove it themselves. They will confirm that it is real, and the number of happy people will increase. A human being is an opportunity. A human being can evolve or degrade. Which way will he goes depends on his awareness and understanding. Nothing should be accepted here based on blind faith alone. You should check and prove everything yourself. You should become aware of everything. If you feel something that causes pain and suffering, jealousy for example, be aware that it is just a mechanical reaction. Once you do become aware of it, you will see that it does not bring you anything good. You need to become aware of this feeling. You need to walk the entire chain of this feeling. You need to become aware of all its manifestations. What kind of thoughts does it cause you to have? What bodily sensations does it bring? You will clearly see how unbalanced you become when you experience these types of feelings. If you were to observe the feeling of anger, you would see what kind of imbalance it introduces into your organism. When you really see all of this, the mechanical reactions that give birth to these feelings will stop. But why do so many people continue to do that? They do that because they are enslaved by mechanical reactions. They perform them without thinking and not even understanding that they behave as mechanisms, as robots.

— *When I become aware of one of such mechanisms, I am afraid to break it. What will I do instead? I caught myself experiencing a negative feeling, and I understood that it was not mine; it was working as a mechanism. I have two questions: "What will I feel if I don't do that anymore? And, if all of this is not mine, then where am I?"*

— Exactly. When we start to see our mechanical reactions, we start to separate ourselves from them. When that happens, you start to feel certain incomprehension. We used to be just the mechanisms repeating the same mechanical actions for a very long time. This mechanicality manifests itself in every sphere: in our thoughts, in our feelings, and in our sensations and actions. Who told you that you need to get upset when someone insults you? Who named this feeling a grudge for you? We receive the definitions of feelings during our upbringing, enculturation, and education by society. They get inculcated into us like a computer program gets downloaded into a computer. Most people don't even question the correctness of the given programs. But if you were to look at different cultures, you would see that cultural stereotypes are very different. What is normal for a Russian man is not normal for an American man. Their stereotypical behavior is totally different from each other. Then what is the right thing to do? One reaction is the correct reaction for a Russian man, while for an American a totally different reaction is appropriate. By the way, people face multiple communication problems because of this discrepancy. Let's look at the sphere of business. For example, when a Russian businessman meets with a businessman from the Western world, he frequently has difficulty making a deal because of completely different cultural traditions. But we are all people. Is there something here that unites all of us? Is there something here that every Russian, Japanese, and American man understands? Is there something here that all of us understand? A singer who performed in many different countries was asked, "What is it that unites all these people you sing for around the world?" He answered, "Love." He sings about love, and people from different countries listen and understand him. He said, "People of different languages understand love. They understand him not because they know the language in which he sings, but because they feel close to what he expresses in his songs. When we orient ourselves to what unites us, we achieve relationships worthy of a Human Being.

Does culture unite or separate us? How many wars occur based on religious grounds? It is paradoxical, but religion is probably one of the most common reasons people kill each other. Don't you find it strange? Jews kill Muslims. Muslim kill Jews. Muslims kill Christians. Christians kill Muslims. What is that? All three major religions talk about God and God's love. Why does war happen? It happens because these people feel neither Love nor God. They just repeat the words, following notions and theoretical concepts. They repeat dead words about their traditions. They teach people how to pray and who to pray to. My God is better than your God. That's what is happening today. A different relationship between people will be possible only once we come to feel and to know what really connects all of us.

Why is it easier to get upset than to love?

— I can understand how the program of "grudge" gets inculcated. Parents get upset with each other, and they show their children how to do it. What about love? It is frequently said that we need to love one another. We can be shown how to do that. Why is it easier for me to get upset and to hold a grudge against my husband than to love him? Why?

— The word "love" became too abstract. The word *love* is used in different situations, and it is used differently by different people. An oppressor approaches a victim and says, "I love you. I am going to hurt you now." An executioner approaches someone and chops off his head also out of love—he loves his profession. This is just his profession—to chop off people heads.

— *People got so entangled in this word. What can connect us if we don't even know what love is?*

— Words themselves separate people. It is not words that are important, but that real thing that stands behind the words. To understand what stands behind the words, you need to go deep inside yourself. You can only come to know the essence of the words you pronounce yourself. Not knowing it yourself, you cannot feel it in word. Much knowledge is based on the opinions of people who frequently don't understand anything. There is also an understanding that is based on personal experience of self-understanding. Many people use the word *love* to describe their desire to make what they want out of another human being. Based on their desires, they say, "I am doing it out of my love for you. It will be good for you. I love you. I know what you need better than you do." That's the way the relationships between many people get built. What does this lead to? It leads to people becoming enemies, or one human being totally controlling and suppressing another, making a floor mop out of him and throwing him out. And this is called "love." Every second phrase during their staying together was, "I love you. That's why I am doing this for you." Is this love? Does it lead to happiness? No, love is something else. But in order to get to know this *something else*, you need to get to know yourself. We need to find the source inside us. This source connects. It does not divide. If what we call love separates us instead of unites us, it is not love. If something, even though it has no name, unites us, it is love. True love opens a human being up and makes him sincere in front of himself and other people.

— *When I have an opportunity to open up and share my thoughts and feelings with other people, I frequently experience fear of rejection.*

— When a human being starts to talk sincerely, not referring to what he read somewhere or heard, many people experience shock. "How can he be so open?" They usually speak very concealingly themselves. "I am not saying that. My girlfriend says that. This is not about me. This is about a friend of mine." Why is a human being so afraid of his own feelings, thoughts, and sensations? Why is it so scary to say that you love someone, if you really feel it? It is very easy to say that if you don't feel it, but very difficult to say if you really feel it. Why is it so difficult for people to talk about something that relates to them personally, and so easy to talk about something or someone who is not related to them?

— *Yes, it is difficult to accept that this is the way things are. Initially, at least, it is very difficult because one is afraid of oneself. One is afraid to see what he harbors inside.*

— When we discover something inside us, we get scared. "Will other people approve of this?" Why are we so afraid to sincerely say something to other people? We are afraid of disapproval. We keep quiet, and we continue to think that we have discovered something bad in ourselves. We think that if we were to talk about it, other people would not approve of us. They will reject us. They will stop being our friends.

"If he leaves me, I will lose everything…"

— Perhaps, you think, "I do not have a close relationship with him now, but at least I have some kind of a relationship. If I sincerely say what I think now, I may lose even that. Yes, I have lived with him for five years already. He actually irritates me, but at least that is some kind of a relationship. If I were to tell him what I feel, he might get angry and leave. In such a case, I will lose even that."

People just want *to survive*. They don't want *to live*. Look at how many shows about survival and different *schools of survival* we have on TV. People don't talk about life; they talk about survival. Let's have what we have, but let's not have war. How long have the Russian people lived in this state, "Anything, but war"? What can we talk about here? What kind of evolution can we even discuss when a man is told, "If you don't do that, it can lead to war"? He says, "Okay. I'll do that. I don't have food to eat. I don't have clothes to wear. But let's hope we don't have another war." This is a great slogan. Who invented it? Where did it come from? The socialist society supported this idea. Both socialist and capitalist societies need this idea. The cold war between Russia and the U.S. was very profitable for the politicians. They scared people with this idea, and scared people are easier to handle. Multiple changes occurred in both countries when the cold war ended. Russia was and still is a shadow of the U.S. Everything negative that happened in the U.S. was projected onto Russia, and vice versa. The American politicians could drop the steam of their problems onto Russia. They used to say, "All of this happened because of the communists." Soviet politicians blamed the U.S. for everything. But when the threat of war with the communists disappeared, the inner quarrels surfaced because

Americans lost their usual channel of garbage disposal. Every society looks for a scapegoat onto which it can project its garbage. This situation occurs in individual relationships, and on the scale of the relationships between countries. For the family which lacks mutual understanding, a scape goat is also necessary. Quite frequently, a family becomes united when its members start to fight against another family. That's the motto politicians have used since the time of antiquity: "Divide and conquer." But this is a vicious circle; it gives birth to the illusion that one should not talk about his feelings and thoughts.

— *I want to return to the question of love again. Why are we so afraid to pronounce the words "I love you"? Love is a feeling that cannot be controlled. I am afraid to tell someone, "I love you" today, because I can lose this feeling tomorrow. But once I have said that, I will feel indebted for life.*

— Let's review what is behind what you have called "indebted for life." Prior to saying something, you may think, "I will say something sincere now, but it can be used against me." If I say, "I love you," I will have to behave accordingly afterwards. Fear appears. Will I want to say it tomorrow? What if I don't? Love is a feeling. A true feeling cannot be subjugated to the control of the mind. As soon as your mind starts to control this feeling or manage it somehow, by using such notions as *have to* and *ought to*, it disappears. The feeling of love cannot exist in an environment of limitations. It can only exist in an environment which is free of limitations and obligations. It appears because it appears, not because someone mandated it to appear.

— *That's why people say that love is suffering. It is impossible not to suffer, being a part of a society and loving at the same time. Multiple*

*responsibilities and the sense of duty press down on a human being, and he
starts to suffer.*

— The traditional society is built on illusory notions, and
as a result, it is not easy to survive in it. If you sincerely feel—it
is abnormal, and you need to be changed to correspond to the
common norms. A human being who understands himself will
say the opposite: "If I cannot freely express what I feel, the
society I live in is not normal."

— *If a human being is strongly attached to his society, he might
think he is not normal himself.*

— Yes. And society constantly ties you to itself using
different means. For example, it maintains your fear but tries
to convince you it wants to remove it. Programs that discuss
threats to people lives are constantly aired on the radio and
shown on TV, and then society says, "You need us. We have
the police. We protect you." Who do you protect us from?
You protect us from ourselves. What is the mafia? The mafia is
a product of society. Society gives birth to another structure
that fights the mafia. It appears that society is one thing and
the mafia another. It appears that policemen are here to
protect us, while in reality, we are dealing with the same
structure. This is a monster of thousands of heads. One head
screams, "I will kill you." Another screams, "Don't be afraid.
I'll protect you." In essence, this is the same monster. People
don't understand that, and they start to do what all these
movie heroes who fight the mafia do—fight the bad guys.
They are doomed, because they are part of society. They fight
themselves. They don't fight a certain, specific mafia. They
fight a certain energy, a certain tendency of society. A
policeman and a thief are two sides of one phenomenon, and it
is not coincidental that they use the same methods that the
mafia uses.

Have you noticed that policemen and mobsters use the same methods? They do that because they are two sides of one coin. When I was young, I saw a great show in one of Moscow circuses. Two men, covered by blankets, were fighting each other for a long time; neither one could get the upper hand. In the end, it turned out that there was only one man there. This image is a good illustration of our conversation. When society starts to disrobe of its many disguises, you can see that you are dealing with the same thing.

Is sincerity a sign of weakness?

— *What about sincerity? Many people consider it to be a weakness. A sincere human being appears to be weak and unprotected. Why is that so? Also, a human being that one opens up to automatically feels stronger. Society itself closes the road to love to its members.*

— Society is not interested in it. Until you understand who is interested in what, you will have difficulty sorting things out. Society is interested in people-automatons who are easy to manage. Let's look at a generic corporation. Most theories of corporate management are based on the principle "stimulus—reaction." That's the easiest way to manage people. It is easier to manage an automaton than to manage a free human being. If you are an army officer and you command a platoon of soldiers, they need to obey your orders. What would happen if the soldiers were to say, "We are not going to do what you order us to do. We are going to go to the movies." What do they do in the army? Soldiers spend most of their time performing meaningless orders. Have you ever wondered why? This is how to create the mechanism of submission and subordination. One can be easily manipulated only when one is totally subdued. Then he can be sent like a pawn to places where he can be easily killed; he will neither object nor protest. We can, of course, think up a beautiful theory about protecting the motherland. But what is the motherland? Look at what happens when people say, "This is my motherland. I will fight for my motherland." Others say, "This is my motherland. I will kill for my motherland." We call it patriotism. This is the way people are brought up. So, why exactly do we kill each other?

— *I want to say something about sincerity again. When one opens up and expresses one's opinion, one becomes active and influential. One closes up in order to defend oneself.*

— Yes, when we say what is acceptable to say, we turn into performers. When a human being says something that is acceptable in the society in which he lives, he is simply a per-for-mer. When he says what he thinks, he is an active personage. In reality, society does not need active personages, it needs performers. An active personage can manifest himself. Such a person acts out of himself, not from the role that was imposed upon him. He acts based on what he feels and considers to be right. When that happens, you start to contradict the role of a performer. You must pay for everything. In order to acquire your own individuality, you will pay by refusing to play the role of a simple performer imposed upon you by someone. It is easy to be a performer. It does not require bravery or strength. But as soon as one starts to manifest bravery and strength, one gets stronger. How can you acquire strength? There is only one way to do that. You must manifest yourself. As you do that, you enter the source of your own power. There is no other way. Otherwise, you are not using your own power; you are using the power given to you by society. It can be taken from you at any moment for insubordination. It is used like a hook that can drag you away at any time.

Someone gives you money and says, "Come tomorrow. I'll give you more." You feel good. You don't have money, and someone gives it to you. Why should you refuse? Then he comes and says, "Today you are going to do this, and tomorrow you are going to do that. You are going to go to this store and beat this guy up. We don't like him. You took money from us. Now you have to do what we tell you to do." You will always have to pay for everything that initially appears to be nice and pleasant. You must pay for everything in this world. You will have to pay for your power by giving up your weakness. People hold on strongly to their weaknesses. To become happy, you will have to pay by giving up your fear. And even though many people say that they want to be happy and rich, in reality, they don't want to part with their sorrow and poverty. You ask, "How come?" The answer is simple. **It is profitable for them to be unhappy**, because when they are unhappy they can ask other people to help them. Look at people who beg for alms at street corners. Many of them have a pretty good life style. Some make a very good living. On what do they build their business? They build it on pity by using different methods. One says, "I am sick. You have to take care of me. Don't you love me? Don't you understand that I can't go to work in my present condition?" — "Okay. Stay home. I'll find a second job. I'll take care of you." People extract a perverted pleasure out of their misfortunes. This leads them to lose their personal power.

Where do your needs come from?

—We just discussed what society does to people. It inoculates them with a certain moral standard, enculturates them, and forces them to follow certain rules. I, on the other hand, constantly return to the root causes. Where is this from? Where is that from? How did that happen? I assert that everything comes from our basic human necessities and our need to satisfy them.

— *Every one of us has certain needs, and if we start to play the games society offers, we do it because society promises to satisfy these needs. If I don't do that, my needs are not going to be satisfied. That's where the roots are.*

— Exactly. Needs are behind everything. We have discussed that a few times already. For example, the field of marketing investigates consumer behavior. The business model of the western world is built upon elucidating different human needs and satisfying them for a profit. It is said that the market follows consumer demands. During the time of socialism, we did not have brothels. There was a demand for them, but we did not have them. Nowadays this demand is being satisfied legally in Russia. A developed society is a society of consumers. It is interested not only in the satisfaction of its consumers, but also in their upbringing. Look at the field of advertising. Its aim is to create certain needs within you. The advertisers who best succeed are paid the most. Smart business people understand this very well. They groom children to be consumers. For example, Coca-Cola finances children's shows, and in the process, inculcates them with their advertisements. A child absorbs the idea that Coca-Cola is the best drink to drink from the crib. Certain needs are formed within people by those who profit from them. These advertisers look after their own benefits. But who determines what these needs are? Who forms these needs, and how do they do it? This is a question we need to ask. Do we really need all the necessities offered by society? This is another question we need to ask. Do we satisfy our real needs in the process? Are we even aware of our real needs?

You can say that they are being satisfied. You can use religious confessions as an example, but take a good look at how this is usually done. Many religions are based on a business model, the only difference being that this business is spiritual. How does a church create its consumers? It asserts that a human being is sinful from birth. You were born sinful. But you are here already, and you must somehow live. Some people don't pay attention to this; others start to wonder why they are so unhappy. Church insists it is due to original sin. And what are you to do with that? You need to go to church and pray for forgiveness. From the business standpoint, it is very profitable to sell indulgences. You have sinned. Now you can buy an indulgence and be forgiven. You can buy a few of them upfront for the future. That's great business. Every human being has spiritual needs. Sometimes we call them conscience. Why does a human being feel a sin? He feels it because a certain notion called conscience has been worked up in him. This notion has been worked up by society. Moreover, what people consider to be sin differs from society to society. What's considered to be a sin in one society quite frequently is a virtue in another. For example, it's a sin to kill a human being, but if he is an enemy killed during a war, it is an act of courage and heroism. But is not this the same thing? The life of a human being was taken. Isn't this the greatest sin? However, our society justifies it. Who started this war? Those in power don't like these questions.

So, our needs are formed in a particular way. The true needs that are present in a human being and lead him toward his evolution are not pursued by most people because society is not interested in them. As a result, billions of dollars are spent to advertise Snickers candy bar, while almost nothing is done to help people understand who they really are, because if people were to understand who they really are, much of what they consider to be super important will stop being so important. Is our society interested in that?

— *You just spoke of different needs: eternal needs and needs that are artificially created. But which needs are primary: material or spiritual? For example, a small boy is told, "Behave yourself"— "What do you mean?" — "Stop running around, sit quietly here." — "I can't do that." — "If you don't stop, you will not get your dinner." The same situation can be played from the spiritual side: "Behave yourself, be quiet." — "I can't." — "In that case, I am not going to love you." In the second example, we are dealing with the need of being accepted which is not being satisfied.*

— We have already spoken of three basic groups of personal needs: the first has to do with safety, the second with pleasure, and the third with power. They are basic. They are the levers by which a human being can be forced to do something.

A human being wants to feel safe. Health and the prevention of different life threats would also fit here. These are the needs that deal with the preservation of the physical body. For example, the needs connected to safety are very strong in Russia. Next, we can separate the needs related to different types of pleasure. For most people, life is based on these basic needs. When a human being constantly lives in a state of fear, he does not see anything else. He cannot think of anything but his personal safety. If you were to scare a cat who is drinking milk, the cat would run away. The cat might have had a need to smell or eat something, but when scared she runs away fast because the need for self-preservation is very strong. This is the most primitive and the strongest need.

73

People who want to control and rule other people usually play on this need.

"Society made me this way..."

— I was brought up the way I was brought up by using levers to control and manage me. Society made me the way I am; the way it needs me to be. What do I do with this now?

— What do you want?

— I don't know. I am asking you.

— You talk about yourself as if from the side. You say, "I was brought up by society." You look at yourself from the side. But who is looking at you from the side? You started to become aware of the fact that you are Peter, and this Peter has certain needs. In reality, these needs were downloaded into you during the process of your upbringing. Who sees this and who understands this now?

— I do.

— And who is this "i"? You, the one who sees it from the side, and you who has all these needs, are different than "i." So, who are you?

— I don't think the meaning is in what we call it.

— The meaning is not in the name we give it, but in our getting to feel and see clearly. When someone comes to you and says, "This is a beautiful thing. Buy it and your prestige will go up." You buy it. But who is buying it? Peter is buying it, the one who was formed by society and who wants to have something prestigious in order to be proud of it. But you can react differently to this offer. Someone offers you something, and you simply become aware of what you think, feel, experience, and do during this process. What does Peter, the product of society, experience? Can you become aware of the

Peter who happens to be the product of the society in which he lives? Can you be aware of what happens to him in different situations? Have you ever done that?

— *I seldom buy these things.*

— I am not talking about any specific thing. I brought it up as an example.

— *I don't buy what is prestigious. I buy things that have practical value. I will never buy an expensive leather jacket. I am happy with a warm, inexpensive parka.*

— It seems to me that you don't understand what I am discussing now. You have asked me, "What do I do now? Who am I?" I am answering your question. You will only be able to understand who you really are when you start to become aware of the way society formed you. Who is this Peter who happens to be the product of society? First, you will understand this. Then you will become aware of this. Finally, in the process of you becoming aware of this, you will turn into the true Peter. The true Peter knows the answers to all these questions. He knows all the answers, but you don't know him yet. I invite you to get to know him, because Peter formed by society got entangled and tied up in the contradictions of society. Life for him is one monotonous movement through the same circles. The answer to your question cannot be received and properly understood by the Peter born by society. Who asks the question, "What do I do now?" If it is asked by the Peter formed by society, he has to do what society wants him to, because he is a product of this society. But if you get outside the borders of this Peter, and you will only be able to do that by becoming aware of your mechanical reactions formed by society, you will get to know a different you—the True you, who knows what to do and how to do it. This True you can answer all your questions. I can talk to you about

75

many things, but you probably will not understand me. It is useless to discuss what I discuss with Peter formed by society, because he would not want to understand. It is also useless to discuss this with True Peter because he knows everything already. So, the only thing I can offer you is to get to know your real you. That's the only thing I discuss.

As you can see, it is not easy to be truly sincere with yourself and others. Let's talk about why we need to do that. Perhaps, you don't even need to be sincere. Perhaps, it is better to hide these things inside yourself and never open up to yourself or others. I am not asking you to walk outside and open your soul to the first guy you meet. I am talking about people who are close to you, people you are in a relationship with and who are important to you. If you cannot say what is important for you to such a human being, it means that you maintain yourself in the illusion that what you feel is horrible and disgusting; he will not understand that, he will disapprove of and reject that. Is not this the main reason for your reticence and secrecy? And if this is the case, then how can you live with this feeling? How can one live while knowing he has something horrible and disgusting inside? But perhaps there is something very important in this that will help you understand yourself. Perhaps this is the only thing that can lead you to understand yourself. Everything else is God-knows-whose, but this is yours. But that is precisely what you are afraid to say; you are maintaining yourself in the illusion that this is something horrible. And that's how you live. Is this a good life? What do you think? In considering something to be horrible and unacceptable, you reject it in yourself. If you cannot talk about it, it means you reject it in yourself. That's how you create a great separation inside yourself. This separation reflects on your inner state and on your whole life.

Friend in the face of an enemy

— *Yes, this separation affects our life. We spend enormous amount of energy maintaining this illusion and hiding what is inside us. This energy can be used to open and to realize ourselves. I want to learn how another human being lives, but I also find it very exciting to share my life with other people.*

— Does it happen often?

— *No, unfortunately it does not happen often.*

— What prevents you from being sincere? Isn't insincerity the main reason behind arguments and conflicts experienced by people who live together? Have you experienced that? Have you been in a situation where you finally expressed everything to him or her and saw the situation resolve as a result? When someone speaks to you sincerely, you can see his true "I." Suddenly, in the face of the enemy, you can see a human being who understands you. That happens when you allow yourself to say everything you wanted to say but were afraid to say to him. Afterwards, you suddenly see the situation resolve. How often have you experienced that in your life?

— *Not often. I would love to see it happen more often.*

— What stands in your way?

— *I think I stand in my own way.*

— Is it a certain part of you?

— *Yes, it is a certain part of me.*

— Look, one of the main errors of a human being is his illusory conviction that "i" is "I", and that this "i" is the only "i." In reality, a human being consists of a multitude of "i"s. One of these "i"s says, "i will always love you." Suddenly, the first "i" is changed by another "i", which says, "i hate you." The third "i" says, "Let's find something interesting to do now." All of this is said by one human being, but in reality, it is said by totally different parts of him, totally different "i"s. The biggest mistake that a man makes is that he thinks that he knows his real "I", while in reality, he mistakes the multitude of "i"s living in his consciousness to be his real "I." A man does not even know one hundredth of his small "i"s Frequently these "i"s are not connected to each other, and that results in inner conflicts. One "i" says, "You need to go and say this." Another "i" say, "No, don't say that." The third "i" laughs, while the fourth one cries. And all of this happens in our inner world. This looks like a lunatic asylum, does it not?

— *We frequently take what is inside us to the wrong people. An illusion is created that we expressed something or acted out one way or another, but frequently all of it goes into the void.*

— An enormous amount of energy is spent maintaining oneself in the illusion of separation. Why am I afraid to honestly express to another human being what I feel and think? It happens because I continue to maintain both of us in the illusion of our separation. But then the only method of communication is to manipulate other people in order to force them to do what one of my small "i"s wants. But this "i" has its opposite "i", which is not going to be satisfied. If I understand that I and another human being are one united whole, I don't need to force anyone, I don't need to manipulate anyone. In this case, we are united by the most amazing and beautiful thing. You can only get to know that if you try.

— *This discovery does not happen automatically. This is a developmental step on the evolution ladder of a human being. When one is closed, one spends a lot of energy to keep oneself closed. At the same time, one also must spend a lot of energy to open up. Afterwards, a lot of energy will be released, but it requires an initial investment.*

— Yes, reclusiveness requires a lot of energy. A free human being starts to understand how much energy he used to spend to be closed. But this is true; to move from the state of reclusiveness to the state of openness you need to have a supply of free energy.

— *Human beings always strive for some kind of a stability, and reclusiveness can be seen as a method to maintain such stability. There is also a certain stability in the creation of an illusion. That's what I recently discovered in me. When I start to open up and to love everyone, I suddenly discover that I don't give a damn about anything.*

— Have you been imitating all of this?

"Do I really hate myself so much?"

— *Yes, I don't understand whether this is my defense or if I really hate myself so much. It is easy to get lost in all of this. How can I separate one from another?*

— We all have different norms. It is inappropriate to speak of love in certain groups. You can't talk about it in jail. To use force is much more appropriate there. People talk about love in brothels, but this is just a form of speech used by people who attend these places. I am talking about something totally different. I am talking about something that is deep inside each one of us. If you start to say, "I love you" left and right, you will soon see that these are just words devoid of any feelings. When, for example, a human being hates someone for a very long time, and then suddenly starts to love him, he just manifests the opposite side of hate. It has nothing to do with true love. This is just an attempt to do what was done before the opposite way. But it is only by getting to know the opposites that you can get to the state of real, not dual love. To understand reality, you must simultaneously see two opposite sides of everything and every situation. The physical world is dual. Everything is dual here: love and hate, poverty and wealth, calm and irritation, etc. If a human being allows himself to see only one side of things, for example to only do the things he believes he should do, he does everything out of *ought to*. Then he suddenly drops everything and says, "I am not going to do anything anymore. I will only do what I want to do." In reality, he stops doing what he did. He is capable of doing only this at that moment, i.e. of doing the opposite of what he did before. Let's say he was constantly told, "Go to work, study, do this." Now he decides, "I don't care for that anymore." He stops going to work. He stops studying, etc. And he says, "I am free now." No. He is as unfree as he was yesterday. He continues to do what he was told to do; he just flipped to the opposite side.

— *It follows that my apathy and indifference are a reaction to my prior desire to get deep into every issue.*

— You are just investigating another side of the same coin. Until both sides of the coin are thoroughly investigated, you cannot enter its center. You must allow yourself what you have not allowed yourself before, but this is not enlightenment yet. Enlightenment occurs when you start to see and accept your opposite parts as a whole. To exit the borders of any duality, you need to investigate both sides of it.

— *I thought this was the limit. This is how I used to deal with people. I didn't give a damn about anything. At some point, I was really sure of that. But when I recall what I did before, I realize that that was also the truth. I understand that both truths are relative.*

— Back then, you behaved a certain way because you believed you should behave that way. Later, you started to behave the opposite way. The old state left you, and you started to explore the state opposite to it. Now you need to see both states inside yourself. We get to know ourselves in oppositions here, on this playground. If we don't allow ourselves to get to know ourselves in some kind of other, not habitual for us side, we get stuck on one side.

— *That means I must observe what is going to happen next, and to work with another side as soon as it starts to manifest itself.*

I know everything, but I don't understand anything

— Yes, you need to observe and experience both sides. Observe that we always push and corner ourselves into one side of a duality by trying to define and name everything. As we define everything that happens to us by using notions that are known to us, the experience that is unknown to us immediately becomes known and familiar to us, even though we neither know nor understand this new experience—we just call it a name. Let's say I experience certain sensations in my body, and I say, "This is pain." This is a completely unusual sensation for me, but I have already defined it with the habitual for me word *pain*. In doing that, I put this new for me sensation into a certain, habitual for me category, and I start to react to it in the same habitual way I react to pain, i.e. I try to get rid of it. I start to take pills or do something to alleviate this new sensation. In reality, this is just a new sensation. By using a habitual word to name this sensation, I start to perform a stereotypical, automatic reaction in relationship to it. **We should not use the words known to us to define the unknown.** To experience without defining is one of the basic qualities of a human being who starts to get to know himself. He does not define new experiences, and he does not put them in the boxes of the old categories. In this way, he is always open to new sensations and experiences. New experiences do not come in the old forms. But when you dress up a new experience in the old names and forms, you kill its novelty. As you correctly observed, most people strive for stability. What does this mean? It means that everything should be known and understood. The mind becomes anxious when it does not understand something. As soon as something unknown shows up, the mind wants to turn it into something it already knows.

Most people do not want to experience anything unknown. Some may be interested in the unknown, but as a rule, they only want to say that they know it already. Only a few people allow themselves to experience something truly new and unknown. Most people simply define it, clip some kind of a tag on it, say that they understand everything, and leave. "I know everything already. I knew it anyway," they say. They want only one thing—to convince themselves and others that they know everything. Yes, they know everything, but they don't understand anything, because they never allow themselves to really understand anything unknown. Many people manifest this behavior. In some people, it is expressed very strongly, in others—less so. As soon as we connect something new with an old notion, we close the opportunity to get to know it. That's why the seeker is similar to a child. He is always open to everything new. He does not try to define anything.

A child does not know anything yet. He has not defined anything yet. That's why he is very interested in the world. He gets to know everything all the time. He wants to feel everything. The adult lives in the closed world of notions, in the prison of the conditioned mind. He has defined, weighed, and put everything in its place. Now he is dying of boredom, but at the same time he is afraid to part with the known. Everything is in the right place, but it is so boring that he wants to hang himself. If you try to move something to another place, he will scream and yell at you; for him, it's a revolution. It's a war for him. Now he considers you enemy number one because his world should be stable and durable. If you try to change something in his world, he will not let you in again. The room he lives in reflects his inner world. God forbid something will be moved there. God forbid something will be taken away.

Your room is your reflection

The room in which a man lives represents the external manifestation of his inner world; it reflects him. The way you treat your clothes and personal belongings also tells a lot about you. Some people save old clothes; others throw old stuff away fast. These tendencies reflect your ability to let go of things that you think belong to you. How do you treat your things? Most people treat their things the same way they treat their thoughts and feelings. Some people cherish their habitual feelings. Let's say you have a feeling of guilt, and you cherish it your entire life. You don't want to part with it. It is old and unpleasant, but it is *familiar*. You don't want to throw it out. If you cherish the feeling of sadness or nostalgia, you will spend your entire life being sad. You don't want to part with it. At the same time, you say, "I want to be happy." I tell you, "Let's throw this old feeling away." You reply, "No!"

What is your relationship with your thoughts? Do you easily part with your notions, convictions, and beliefs? For most people, it is very hard because their habitual world view breaks. They want stability, but later, this stability brings them to things they were so afraid of, such as diseases and suicide. Life is fluid. Everything floats. Once you understand that, you start to move toward yourself, and eventually you come to a point when you start to see your life as a flowing river. You will see that everything flows; something comes and something goes. You will not be attached to anything. A thought will come and go. A feeling will come and go. A sensation will appear and turn into another sensation. You will start to see and understand that *you* are not this thought, feeling, or a role to play. You are not the body you inhabit either. You are something entirely different, great, and unified with everything else. This state cannot be defined; it can only be felt and experienced. You can only come to your center when you observe and are aware of yourself. When you finally get there, you will relate to everything that surrounds you differently. You will enjoy everything and not try to hold on to anything.

Should one fight for the happiness of another human being?

— *Let's take a look at family life. I work on myself and go deeper and deeper, but my husband does not want to work on himself. He does not want to evolve. I asked him to join me, but he does not want to do that. He says he is fine the way he is. What should I do? Should I accept this and work on myself for as long as is necessary to accept that he does not want to work on himself? Should I do it for the family's sake, or should I keep trying to wake him up, so he will join me?*

— The most horrible crimes were committed in the name of great ideals. The Crusades that took so many lives were lead in the name of God. You can ruin yourself and others for the family's sake. What is a vendetta? My family was insulted, and I must avenge it. In the mountains of Italy and Georgia, a man will be condemned by his village if he does not kill the man who insults a member of his family. How did the mafia appear? The mafia was built on the idea of the superiority of a family, i.e. of a certain group of people. An individual human being is of little importance there; the traditions of his family are paramount, and to maintain these traditions, people kill other people.

I call you toward *spiritual egoism*. Learn, develop, and evolve only for yourself. Many people try to do something for the sake of other people. Look where it leads them. "I live for my children," a woman says. Where does it lead her? Later, kids run away from her, and the only thing they remember is tough times. I get suspicious when someone says, "I do this for my children's sake. I do this for my husband's sake." I suspect insincerity. When I look at the life of people for whose sake it is being done, I see that it is horrible. In reality, "I do it for someone's sake" is just a slogan. You don't do anything for anyone's sake. You just try to do something for someone that you did not want to do and do not want to do for yourself. For example, if you have not received college education, you will try to motivate your kids to get one. You project your unsolved problems onto them. They have their own lives to live, and they have their own aims, but you don't allow them to understand and to solve their own assignments, forcing them to solve your unsolved problems. Please, solve your own puzzles, and everyone will feel better. If the human being next to you does not share your point of view, it is quite likely that you don't understand what you want yourself. You say that you are walking the spiritual path, but quite likely you are trying to use some of the knowledge you received to manipulate other people for your egoistical interests. You used to tell him, "Do this, because I want you to do this. I need you to do this." Now you are telling him, "Do that because God wants you to do that." But it is not God who wants that, it is you. You just use God's name to force someone to do what you need in order to feel good. Many people do that. You are not alone.

For example, the church blesses people to go to war. It did that a thousand years ago, and it continues to do so. What kind of God are we dealing with if priests use his name to bless their parishioners to murder other people? Whatever you do, you need to do it for yourself, for your inner awareness and growth. When you finally get to know who you really are, people's reactions toward you will change. You will not have to force them to do anything. They will understand everything themselves. A man says, "I want to understand God. I think I already understand God." He just started to read the Bible yesterday, and he already understands everything. He walks around telling people about God and the fact that he understands God and how to follow him. And he is very surprised when other people don't understand him, don't pay attention to his words, or start to argue with him. He says, "Why? I understand God. They should listen to me." In reality, he doesn't understand anything. He just uses God's name to do what he did before and to rub his vanity. When a man really understands something, he does not need to talk about himself. People start to talk about him. They say, "He understands something very important, and I want to understand that too." Once you start to understand things, people will come to you and ask, "How do you live? Why do you live the way you live? How can you feel life so well?" They will come to you. You will not have to force them to listen to you.

Why doesn't he want to understand you?

— *When you live with a man, you have to talk to him. It's good to share silence, but sometimes you need to talk too. We have our own notions, and we introduce our own meaning by choosing the words we use. Sometimes, it is difficult to find a common language.*

— A human being who tries to understand himself starts to perceive many things differently, and he wants to share his discoveries. However, the people next to him frequently do not understand him. This is not easy. To feel another human being is an art. If you discuss something that you think is important for him, but he does not need it at that moment, most likely you just want to show off how knowledgeable you are, or you want to get rid of the garbage you have accumulated. In this case, his natural reaction will be to reject you. On the other hand, if you feel something inside yourself and talk about it with another human being, you talk about yourself. You talk about yourself, not about him. But if you, feeling something inside, project it onto another human being, it means you don't understand anything. "Something happened to me yesterday, and I realized that you don't love me. You don't accept me. You never loved me. You have never accepted me," you say. You think you are very sincere, and you are surprised when his reaction to your words is to get nervous. What is happening here? You understood something about yourself, and you saw that he also has the same understanding. You understood that he and you are one, and you started to emphasize this with him. You say, "Yesterday I felt how unjust I was to you. I did not understand many things. What I used to ask of you was not fair. I did not realize that you have your own needs. I understand that now." He will look at you differently. He will say, "This is true. How did you find this out?" That's when he will get interested and make a step toward you. He will say, "I have not treated you right a few times too. I wanted to force you to do what I did not do myself." **We always talk about ourselves, but in the process of doing that, we try to talk about other people and to advise them.** You need to become aware of this. But if we start to talk about ourselves, we will see people's attitude toward us change. Perhaps, someone will say, "You understand something. I thought about it for a while, but I never spoke about it ..."

— *I did that a few times, and I felt malice coming from my partner. "You finally accepted that it was you. You used to say that this was me!" That was his reaction.*

How do you say what you say?

— Everything depends on how you say what you say. Based on what you say now and how you say it, I can infer **how** you said what you've said to him.

— *I speak of my own mistakes.*

— Mistakes can be either accepted or not. The timbre of your voice, your pose, and your body language carry a lot. For example, I can say, "I understood that what I did before was not right. You have the right to live your life the way you want to ..." I say the correct words. You can write them down and read them. Everything was said correctly. But how did I say them? Which feeling is behind them? Do I force myself to pronounce every word as if I was letting a poisonous snake out?

Try to look deeper inside yourself. Based on my experience, if your words are sincere, people will react to you differently. They might be shocked, and they might yell at you first. But they will start to understand something. When you start to change, people who are close to you will start to change too. It's impossible for them not to change. The process of change will be slow and painful, but it will occur.

— *The most important thing is patience, right?*

— Yes, you have to have patience. These people lived their entire lives fighting each other. They will need time to change this stereotypical behavior. Sometimes it happens fast. One example is when a human being experiences a very stressful situation, such as a near death experience. What are you willing to pay for this understanding? What are you willing to sacrifice? If you become aware of your problem and want to solve it fast, you must sacrifice something. Do you have enough strength to do this? You can burn your karma in an instant, but it will be accompanied by heavy suffering. We can look at Jesus's crucifixion from this point of view. It is impossible for a human being living on earth to not have karma. Even Jesus Christ had karma. And for him to leave this world, he had to burn it. Crucifixion can be seen as a very fast way of transforming karma. This is enormous suffering, but is burns karma and frees a human being of his dependencies and of the mandatory return to this playground. Everything depends on what you choose. If you want to burn your karma fast, you will have to experience great suffering. Are you ready for that? If you are not, this will happen at a slower speed.

Emotional traps

— Can you feel the problems of other people with loving compassion? Can you avoid being emotionally dragged into their traps? What do I mean by this? Let's say someone starts to complain to you about his life. He says, "This is horrible.

The country is going God knows where. My wife left me. I am getting sick. My mother is dying. My kids are sick all the time." People complain of many things. Why did this man come to you? What does he want from you? He came for you to pity him.

— *He wants to get something from me.*

— He wants to get energy from you through pity. If you pity him, you will help him maintain the illusion of separation. You will help him maintain the illusion that everything is wrong with the world. You will fool yourself and you fool him. He came to you saying, "Look how bad things are. Everything is horrible. Listen to the radio. Watch the TV. Listen to what people are saying." And if you were to do that, you would find it to be true: everything is horrible, and it will even get worst pretty soon. He wants to awaken your pity through this. These people feed on the habitual energy of pity, which reinforces their usual state. Now we have two people who share the illusion that everything is wrong with the world. If everything is wrong here and we live in a horrible world, what can we do but whimper? And why don't we steal if everything is so bad? Why don't we kill someone if it is so bad? Why shouldn't we behave this way if the world is so bad? People spread this poison around. This poison forms and reinforces their illusion that something is wrong with the world. The world is quite all right. Life is wise! But if one does not understand that, one sees the world as a horrible place. If a human being understands himself, he sees the world as a loving and wise place. The world creates multiple opportunities for a human being to understand who he really is and to come to understand unity, happiness, and love. This is how this world is made. It is made to help a human being to understand that. But when we support other people in their illusions of separation and give into this notion ourselves, we lose the true meaning of this world.

From suffering to compassion

I suggest you relate to other human beings with compassion, but without getting into the trap of pity and condemnation. What does it mean to relate to someone with compassion? It means to understand that the man sitting in front of you crying and complaining experiences a difficult period of his life. You have been in these states, and you know what they are. But the fact that he feels bad, was insulted, robbed, or is experiencing some physical ailment does not mean that something is wrong with the world. The world is Okay, and this man has been offered an opportunity to understand something very important right now. And what happens to him now is the best way for him to understand that. You need to tell him that. You need to help him understand that he has a great opportunity to understand something very important about himself. You should not sit with him crying. No, you should be calm, totally calm. This calmness comes as the result of your understanding that everything is right and beautiful! Here he is crying and screaming, and this is beautiful. He just does not see this beauty yet. You see it. You see a new opportunity in his current state. If you don't see it yet, you will tell him, "Why are you so upset? Everything is good." You have not felt it yet and you don't understand it yet, but you are trying to prove it to him. Don't be surprised by his response, "Are you an idiot?!" If you don't understand it yourself, you will not be able to show it to him. If you understand it, you don't even need to express it in words; everything will be clearly visible based on

91

your inner state. He is very upset about the situation, and you are calm. And then a question appears in him, "Why is he so calm?" He might become interested in what you have that allows you to be calm. Look at all these people who try to force others to believe in God. They are usually not very successful. Why? They are not successful because they are not the manifestation of divinity themselves. They react to what happens around them the same way as those whom they try to talk some sense into. They just talk about God. In reality, they react to everything exactly the same way. As a result, these people believe neither themselves nor the God they peddle. But when one maintains awareness, acceptance, and love in every state, he is an example of a different quality of life. In this case, many people develop a desire to find out why and what happened to you. And if you tell them, "I know God", they might become interested. They may think, "What kind of a God gives him such strength?" They may want to get closer to this God. It will not work any other way. If you say that your life differs from the life of others, when in reality, it is the same, people will not believe you. And they will be right. For them to believe you, you need to understand yourself and to be aware.

You will have to deliver yourself

— *I want to ask you a question. Should I help another human being to understand these new opportunities, or he should have to experience them himself?*

— Life provides a human being with the best opportunities. How can you help a man to experience them? It is impossible; you can never help another human being. A human being can only help himself. You can understand something on your own. A woman can give birth to her child only by herself. No one can give birth for her. But it is possible to help a woman who is about to deliver. How? You can make sure she is well fed. You can take care of her and make sure she is not nervous. You can assist her during the process of delivery. This is real help, but no one can deliver for her. So, you can only help if you understand what's going on correctly. A wise man is a man who came to understand himself in all his manifestations. How can you understand someone who is about to deliver a baby if you have not delivered yourself? It is not coincidental, for example, that the society of Alcoholics Anonymous was formed by those who went through and healed themselves from alcoholism. They understand people who suffer from alcoholism better than anyone else because they have been there themselves. They went through it themselves. The average man sees the alcoholic as a sick and filthy human being. The average man does not understand what an alcoholic man experiences, why or how he became what he is, and what is delirium tremens. How can you understand a man who drinks himself to death, if you have not been drunk yourself? Only those who have had a similar experience, who entered it and got out of it, can understand him. When you encounter problems that you have solved yourself, you will feel compassion toward those who are going through similar problems now. And you will be very tactful and attentive to them. If, on the other hand, you have never felt what they experience, you are unlikely to understand them. Most people try to teach others or to help them. Usually their help consists of demands, "You should do this! You should not do that!" A man replies, "I can't stop drinking." And he is told, "You should not be drinking!" They don't understand each other, and as a result, they scream at each other. The one who went through this experience will not do that. He will just empathize and softly help the other human being to go through his life experience on his own.

— *It seems to me that there is a natural way to help someone understand something. If you communicate with a man for a long time, eventually you will see something in him that he does not see himself or is afraid to acknowledge. I can simply show him a different reaction to the part he denies in himself. I can tell him, "I see this in you, but this is intrinsic to every human being." I can show him that I react to him differently, and he will understand that there is a way to get rid of his inner problems.*

— Yes, this is really important. When a man, who has always felt that people see him as someone sick and deranged, suddenly realizes that one human being see him differently, he starts to see himself differently. Why is it so difficult for people to understand what true love is? It is difficult for them because they have never been truly loved. Suddenly someone, who relates to him differently from everybody else, shows up. Initially, he does not understand what's going on. Then he starts to think that this is not bad, and eventually he starts to relate to himself in the same fashion. You can really change a man this way, by relating to him in a way that he himself cannot relate to himself yet. But to relate to him in this way, you need to see his real face. You need to look deep into his soul. It is not coincidental that people say that if you manage to see Jesus Christ in a man and Mother Maria in a woman, you will see the true essence of a human being. If you see the Mother of God in a street woman, you will not scream at her or insult her. It would be impossible. You can insult and kick a human being only if you see something mean and nasty in him. When you see something divine in a man, you cannot relate to him in such a fashion. If you manage to see something beautiful in a human being, he might find it amazing at first, but then he will start to relate to himself the same way. You can come to understand something only through your own experience. Wise are those who have not only experienced a lot, but who also understood and became aware of what they experienced. Many people have gone through war. They have experienced what people usually don't experience in daily life. And what happened to them? Some of them understood something very important about themselves. Others became mean; they want to avenge themselves and kill. Some returned as well-prepared killers; for them it was a preparatory school. They have passed the threshold of killing, understood the horror of it, and became professional killers. The opportunities life provides are not coincidental, and what you extract from them depends on you and on you only. It depends on your level of consciousness.

Do you want to receive everything without doing anything?

— *Many people pray to God asking to solve their problems. The way I understand it, God can help, but you must make the first step. I have tried helping many people throughout my life, but unless they did something on their own, my help was useless. I want to say that people must do something on their own.*

— Only a human being can make a choice, and that is what separates a man from animals, plants, and minerals. They have no choice. Born a tree, a tree lives as a tree. Born an animal, an animal lives as an animal. But born a human being, a man has the opportunity to evolve. A human being is a limitless opportunity.

— I recalled two interesting situations that happened to me. Once, I went to a sorcerer and asked him to help me become successful. He gave me an amulet and asked me to repeat a certain prayer. Two days later, I signed a very important and amazing contract. I could have worked there for a year, but because I did not use it correctly, it was ruined. Two months later, I went to church. I prayed for two months, and I landed even a better contract. Unfortunately, I was unable to use this opportunity either. I was unable to use God's help properly.

— People have an interesting notion of God. They see God as a middle level manager who can do everything but who asks to be paid back. I will pray to God, and God will give me what I want. Many people pray because they want to get something. It is some sort of a business deal. I prayed to you for eight hours, and I expect three hundred dollars in return. I prayed to you for twelve hours, and I expect five hundred dollars. That's how many people think. This is a simplified and disfigured notion. At the same time, it is also true that you must pay for everything here. I remember a good movie called *The Evenings Spent on the Village of Duhanka.* A man sells his soul to the devil. Do you remember how it ends? He goes crazy at the end. Yes, you can use the help of certain creatures to satisfy your egoistical desires. Some of them are impatiently waiting for you to do that. They will give you anything you want as if for free. You make a deal. You sell your soul, and you are given some material goods in return. It seems to you that this is great; you are getting everything for free. That's what most people dream of—to do nothing and to receive everything. This is their idea of happiness. But that's not what life is about. You will have to pay for everything, and for some things you will have to pay quite a steep price.

You will have to pay for everything that you have done without getting your soul into it. You can only help yourself.

Only your own effort can help you. You cannot ask for anybody's help here, and if you are provided with such "help" you must watch out—you will have to pay for it, and the price will be steep.

An old joke comes to mind. A new Russian walks down the street and sees a very expensive Mercedes. He develops a strong desire to possess it. Suddenly, he hears a voice: "I will get it for you, but you will have to give me your soul in exchange." "Okay. But where is the catch?" — the guy replies happily.

Be vigilant with people who offer you free help. Quite frequently, it is not easy to understand what motivates people to do that. Learn to separate people who offer anything to you from their heart from people who have a hidden agenda. Their external behavior may appear the same. Why does a human being offer you something? Have you thought about that? Why do certain people offer you something without asking anything in return? Why do they do that? If they ask you to pay for it or to be respected for it, it is common and is therefore an understandable behavior. But why do some people do something for *free*, or for its own sake?

Is the additional payment for love necessary?

— *Perhaps, they do it out of some kind of need of which they are unaware?*

— What is unaware need? For example, a woman has loved her child for many years and she was not aware of it. Suddenly, this **unawareness** leads her to say, "I was taking care of you my entire life. I am old now. You must take care of me now." And she starts to reproach her son every time he does not do what she wants him to do. The comeback may come eventually, but it will always come. What appeared to be unselfish in the beginning may wind up being very selfish in the end. So, this so-called **unaware "love"** may turn into a huge profit. Everything a human being does subconsciously, without awareness, will later manifest itself in some form of a complaint or demand.

— *I don't remember people doing anything for me without some kind of self-interest. One way or another, they always ask for something in return.*

— Yes, no one does anything for free in this world. You must pay for everything here. This principle works everywhere and all the time. Imagine a man who loves to dance. He feels good when he dances. He experiences great pleasure from it. He comes to a dance floor and he dances. He is a great dancer. If he was to dance this well at the Bolshoi, the administration would have charged a hundred dollars per ticket to see his performance, while here he just smiles and says thank you after the performance. He does not ask for a payment. He has already received it. When a man does something that gives him pleasure and happiness, he does not need additional payment. He receives great pleasure and happiness in the process.

Such a man does not ask to be paid for his work. Money come to him as the result of natural rather than artificial exchanges with other people. When a human being does something he is not happy to be doing, he insists on being paid for his services. If a human being does something out of happiness, people develop a desire to share something with him, to give him something, whether it is bread, money, or something else. This desire appears in them naturally. He does not need to ask for anything. That's where the secret lies. We constantly say, "A man should somehow get money to maintain his body." This is true. But based on this statement, many people conclude that they need to look for some kind of job that they would be paid for. Therefore, one must ask to be paid for his work. When you are occupied with a job you don't love, you demand money for your work. When you do what you love and do it well, people thank you. In this case, such phrases as *have to*, *ought to*, or *must* disappear. There is no more *have to* there, but only *love*. And the amount of money and other material goods, if we were to talk about it, will increase. When you demand love from someone, you only receive a surrogate. If you really love a human being, he or she will return your love.

"I do it to be loved..."

— *I want to share what I became aware of during this seminar. To my horror, I became aware of the fact that when I do something for someone, when I give something to people without asking anything in return, I try to convince myself and others that I do it unselfishly, because I am good. I realize now that I do it because I want them to love me. By giving something to people, I want to receive their love, even though I am not aware of it. Why I want to receive their love is another question.*

— Quite a lot is buried under the word *love*. Many people equate it with prestige, attention, respect, etc. Those are different things, but people use the same word to describe them. For example, "I want people to pay attention to me. I am not asking for anything else. Just look at me and talk to me." Another man says, "It is not enough for me just to have your attention. I want you to acknowledge that I am the smartest and the strongest here..."

— *There is something else here. Let's say, I help someone while not expecting to get anything in return. I do it because I feel a connection with*

99

this man. When I brush my teeth in the morning, for example, I don't think that I do it for someone else; I think that I need it myself. When I cut my hand, I take care of it. In the same way, when I see that someone needs my help, I perceive him or her as my hand.

— If you feel that way, then you understand that we are one unified organism. And if I see that one part of me needs something, I will assist that part. I will do that not because I expect to be paid back, but because we are one whole. If some part of me is hurting, I hurt. God feels everything and everyone. When someone suffers, God suffers with him. Christ's crucifixion continues every minute because he continues to carry the pain of the entire human race. When we understand that, we can understand why such a being wants humanity to change. He wants us to change because his pain is our pain, because He and We are One. We are not dealing with any gain or profit here. We feel compassion for everything. The only way for such a being to get rid of suffering is to make sure that the whole organism feels good, and that every part and organ of it experiences love, not suffering. And if God sends his messengers for humanity to start seeing its life differently, it is only done because He and We are One.

— *When I discuss these things with my friends, I frequently hear this retort: "But I cannot help everyone." I tell them that nothing happens coincidentally; life offers different types of help, but many of us reject it.*

— A man is swimming in the ocean after a shipwreck, screaming, "Help! Help!" A boat passes him by, and people tell him, "Climb aboard." He replies, "No. I am waiting for God. God will save me. God, please help me!" Finally, he drowns and gets to heaven. Standing in front of God, he asks, "Why didn't you save me? I believed in you. I was asking for your help, but you..." — "I sent a boat your way," God replies. Help comes in the form of different people in our lives, and if we don't see the Divine intervention, that is our problem. We say, "I will accept help from you. I will not accept help from him. He is not God's servant because he is dirty and dressed shabbily. God's helper cannot look like that. He should wear an Armani suit. He should speak well and smell good." To empathize with someone is not to start playing a role of a supporting actor in his show. Many people get caught in this role. For example, someone complains, and you start to complain with him or to feel pity for him. In this way, you support his illusory role. People used to hire professional mourners in ancient Rome. This profession is still available here.

What does the state you are in communicate to the people around you?

— You can act freely when you are aware, when you are in your essence. When you are anxious, excited, and beside yourself, you can only give birth to the same states in others. We are discussing some novel ideas now. Let's say you have memorized them, but while going back home on a bus, someone steps on your foot or a thief pinches the wallet out of your pocket. You come home in a totally different state, but you still remember what we have discussed. You try to discuss these ideas with your spouse or your friend. You are angry, and you want to hit someone, but you try to be nice, all knowing, and show some empathy instead. You start to discuss these new ideas while not being in a harmonious state. Do you think people will understand you? What will your words convey? **When someone is beside himself, everything he says, feels, and does is disharmonious and unconvincing. Therefore, before you talk to someone about something,**

you need to bring yourself to a calm and centered inner state. That's the essence of our work. As soon as you feel irritation, you need to increase your awareness of your state. You need to constantly observe your inner states. People track down what they say, how they say it, where they go, and what they do. These are external things. The results of your actions, however, will depend on your inner state. You bought a good present for your friend while feeling very angry. What will this present bring to him? It will bring him anger. Don't be surprised if you feel nauseated after eating an apple, if the man who sold you the apple from is constantly irritated. His state was transmitted to you through the apple you ate. The state we are in while we are doing something is extremely important. Actually, it is not what we do but the state we are in while we do what we do that is of most importance. What's important is not what we say but the state we are in when we say it. To be aware of our inner state is very important in our work. I constantly remind you of that: "Be aware! Be aware of your thoughts! Be aware of your feelings! Be aware of your sensations!" Let's say you came to someone and you started to say something mechanically. Suddenly, you recall the question I pose to you every time we meet. You ask yourself, "What do I feel now?" and you see that you feel irritation. You observe your state, and it changes. You need to do this all the time. You need to experience this. By becoming aware, you become calm. In this case, everything will proceed well and harmoniously. You must constantly observe the state you are in. Don't judge it. Don't try to define it. People are afraid to be coughed at. They are afraid of getting infected. It is good to be externally clean, but external cleanliness is insignificant when compared to the dirt that is transmitted through words, moods, and actions. The viruses of irritation, jealousy, and fear can be transmitted very fast. The only way you can stop these infections is to shift your attention inside and to observe your states.

— *I was in such a crazy state earlier, but you've said, "Stop! Observe!", and I have experienced this. What you have just discussed is really true. I am in a totally different state now. I am calm and balanced.*

— Great. It is sometimes necessary to scream at a man in order for him to become aware of himself. Some people consider it strange. In one of his novels, Russian author Turgenev described a man who spoke for two hours. He was unable to stop. His friend had to break a lamp in order to switch him to a different state.

Who wants to share his experience of awareness? What happens when you start a conversation while being stressed and anxious? How does it usually end? How often do you observe your inner states?

— *I have not felt angry or been upset in the last six months. If I buy apples from an angry guy, I know how to clean them. One can buy* angry *apples and clean them up.*

Where do the seeds of suffering grow?

— If you are in a state of total awareness, you can do anything you want—you can drink water from a dirty puddle. Nothing will happen to you. This is not about the apples. This is about your state. If you eat the apples contaminated by the anger of a man who sells them, when you are in the angry state, these apples will resonate with your state. Whatever you have in you will grow. No one can cause a man to experience a state that is not in him. Any given disease *sprouts* on a corresponding soil. If a man gets sick with the flu, it means he was ready to get sick with the flu. A virus finds a soil it likes.

You can't get weeds to grow on asphalt; it needs soil. Things only grow in the soil in which they *can* grow. The soil for different negative emotions is successfully prepared in many people. It is being constantly cultivated. People cultivate soil for each other, so the seeds of anger, hatred, fear, and jealousy can grow in them. We need to spend more time cultivating the soil where understanding, awareness, and Unconditional Love will grow. Everything needs to be prepared. What can grow on unploughed soil? Only weeds. But if you have prepared the soil properly, everything you sow will sprout and grow well. Therefore, before we start to understand ourselves, the soil must be prepared. And when the soil is prepared, the sower will come, sow the seeds of wisdom, and they will produce fruit. But the soil must be prepared well by you. That's what we do here. We prepare our inner soil. The process is not simple. Look at how farmers prepare their fields for sowing. This is hard, important work on which the harvest and future fruits depend.

— *My personal experience supports that. When I feel centered and filled with energy, I can do anything I want. A sense of rightness appears, and everything flows smoothly. When I am not centered, I doubt myself and move from side to side. Nothing goes right. I have learned to discern when I am in this state and when I am not. But how can I maintain this state, and what can I do when I feel that it is leaving me?*

Understanding is knowledge without doubt

— When you really understand, you don't doubt. You don't need to ask anymore, "Do I understand it correctly or not? Do I do this correctly or not?" When true understanding comes your way, the question of whether it is right or wrong does not appear. You simply understand that this is it. You don't need any confirmations. When a man asks you about something, it means he is not sure. The one who understands does not ask questions. He doesn't need confirmation. It was Galileo who said that Earth moves around the Sun. When the inquisition found out about this, he was threatened and advised to refute his words. He was an old man, and he got scared. But he knew the truth. He recanted, but as he rose from his knees, he murmured, "It still moves." True knowledge does not change irrespective of what people say about it, whether they support it or not. True knowledge will remain true irrespective of whether people understand it or not. And when true knowledge enters a human being, he knows that it is true. Calmness comes at that moment when a human being understands and becomes aware of himself and of what's happening around him. Thoughts may come afterwards: "It came and it went. I don't know when it will come again." Like a traveler who finds a water well, he wants to drink and drink. He wants to fill himself with water for the rest of the way, as he does not know when or if he will see another well. He will fill up a few bottles and carry them carefully. He will use this water very sparingly. He may save it for himself and try not to show it to anyone. Our situation is different. If a human being really walks the way of understanding, his source is endless. He will have a limitless source of energy. The question of energy is a question of awareness. When you are aware, the energy comes your way. As soon as you stop being aware, you lose it. Everything depends on the level of your awareness.

— *I agree with you. I don't have any questions. I have experienced many situations during my life that confirm that what you say is true. I know that everything that is being discussed here is true, but I don't live like that all the time. What prevents me from doing that? I need to constantly remind myself. I need to constantly redirect attention inside and to be aware. It is very difficult. And when Peter was saying that he feels good when he has energy, I recalled that at some points in life I did not have it, but I was able to change something in me and it reappeared. It usually happens when I am with people. I say something, and then I understand that what I said was nonsense. I have no idea why I said it. I don't see the human being I am talking to. Some of these situations were totally incomprehensible. Yesterday, I was able to explain something to a man with whom I am living. I did not expect that of myself. When that happened, both of us got in a great mood. We were filled with energy. For him, it was something new and amazing.*

From knowledge to understanding

— Exactly. What we are discussing, and we have discussed it quite a few times, becomes known to you. But to what extent do you really understand this? It is one thing to know something on the level of words and ideas. It is a totally different thing to experience and to understand it. For knowledge to convert to understanding, an extensive work directed to becoming aware of yourself in different situations of your life is necessary. As most people do not want to do this, their knowledge does not convert into understanding. The process of evolution stops for these people. We need a new system of education, and I offer you one. It is not the traditional, academic education, which accents the accumulation of information and the ability to use it for some personal gain. This kind of knowledge overburdens a human being, as it is frequently not confirmed by one's own life experience. The enormous quantity of knowledge that a human being receives during his lifetime is not confirmed by his own experience. This is especially true in spiritual, psychological, religious, esoteric, and philosophical spheres.

Everyone should learn what he does not yet know. Someone needs to learn to be more active, while someone else needs to learn to be passive. This is just one example. I can offer you many more. Therefore, the system of education should be geared toward converting knowledge into understanding, which only happens when one becomes aware of oneself. For a human being to have the necessary for him opportunities of personal experience, they should be created. Then they must be experienced and understood correctly. This is the base that will allow you to get to know and to become aware of yourself. **I call it holistic psychology, or the psychology of getting to know oneself as a certain mechanism, i.e. getting to know your mechanical reactions to exit their borders and to achieve wholeness.** And as every human being has a great many mechanical reactions, their elucidation requires time, attention, and quite a detailed work. This is the only approach to education that will allow you to truly understand yourself.

— *I want to share my experience of awareness. A certain man was causing me to experience negative emotions. It took me two weeks to become aware of what was behind it. I understand now that I see in him what I don't want to see in myself—my anger. It is buried very deep. When someone tells me something and uses the word* anger, *I feel very uncomfortable. I understand now that I have tried to be nice all my life, while in the process, I was very angry. I was afraid to acknowledge this to myself all along.*

— Congratulations!

— *I feel ashamed of myself.*

— Great! Your next assignment is to become aware of shame.

What's really going on?

— *It is precisely other people who help us to see ourselves from a side. For example, for a very long time I could not understand how you influence me. Why do certain processes get activated inside me? Now I understand that when a certain human being can express and verbalize my thoughts, I can look at them from the side.*

— *It was very important for me to understand that as soon as one starts to open up to other people, one starts to better understand oneself. It is not only you who give something to people. It turns out that people want to give something and share something with you too. I receive great pleasure from this. I want to learn to give and to receive what other people can give me.*

— *I want to thank you, Alexander Alexandrovich, and everyone here. I have received a great present today. I realize now how important it is to get deep inside myself and to communicate from that level. I have experienced closeness with all of you today. I want to thank you for this.*

— *Today I feel that I am me. Quite frequently, I feel the opposite state. It usually appears in official buildings: police stations, military offices, law firms, and court houses. I feel like a puppet on a string. It is a very unpleasant state.*

— *I want awarenes to become the guiding light that will not allow me to drown in the sea of illusions.*

— *This is not my first time here. Every time I come, I perceive things differently. It's almost as if different parts of my organism perceive different things each time. Last year it was different. I feel fuller now, as if many things got to the right places inside me. This brings me closer to the calmness and harmony we are discussing now.*

— Look how great it is when knowledge converts into understanding. It appears that we talk about the same thing again and again, but every time we come to understand it deeper and deeper because we allow ourselves to be honest. Each one of us changes the human being next to ourselves. This work can only be done together. You can only become aware of yourself through others.

— *This is very interesting, and the theme we discuss is endless. It can be reviewed from many different angles.*

— The life of a human being is an endless story. It never starts and never ends. This is the beauty of it.

— *I have not been working for two years because at one beautiful moment I understood that what I did before stopped bringing me pleasure. I had a certain amount of money saved, but I am running out now. My friends and business partners advise me to return to the work I did before—to sell oil—but I keep asking myself the same question: would I have done it if I was not paid for it? Today I received the answer to my question. I was right. I've declined to return to this work for the last two years, and I will decline it again. I feel certain that something interesting will come in the end that will not only bring me money, but will also bring me pleasure.*

— *I felt bad throughout the seminar. I could not sleep most of the time. I was very restless. I feel very good now. I want to thank everyone.*

— I want to remind you that in order to awake, you need to have a good sleep. Some people need to spend many lives asleep.

— *Some people say that one works in order to feed oneself. I think the most important thing is to find the right place in life. In that case, both the material and spiritual things will come to you. One should not disrespect the material side of life.*

— This devision of things onto material and spiritual is just another illusion of separation. Material things are dense. What do dense things consist of? If we were to dig deeper and deeper, we would come to the unified energy of love that this entire world is made of. Then we will see that the material things represent spiritual things, and vice versa.

CHAPTER 4
RELATIVES.
DIFFICULTIES IN RELATIONSHIPS

Your children are not your children.
They are the sons and daughters of Life's longing for itself.
They come through you but not from you,
And though they are with you yet they belong not to you.

You may give them your love but not your thoughts,
For they have their own thoughts.
You may house their bodies but not their souls,
For their souls dwell in the house of tomorrow,
which you cannot visit, not even in your dreams.
You may strive to be like them,
but seek not to make them like you.
For life goes not backward nor tarries with yesterday.

You are the bows from which your children
as living arrows are sent forth.
The archer sees the mark upon the path of the infinite,
and He bends you with His might
that His arrows may go swift and far.
Let your bending in the archer's hand be for gladness;
For even as He loves the arrow that flies,
so He loves also the bow that is stable.

—Kahlil Gibran, *The Prophet, On Children*

Close distance fight

— Why is it so difficult for us to communicate with our relatives and the people who are close to us? Why do most serious and difficult conflicts appear in relationships with blood relatives and people we choose to live with? It is precisely in these close relationships that the shadow sides and features of our personality, which cause suffering, manifest themselves strongly.

— *We spend most of our time with these people. They see us from every side. We open up to them. We communicate all the time. Sometimes, we can't even get away from them when we want to.*

— Exactly. They are close. One cannot get away from them. They are always by your side, whether you are in a good mood or a bad mood. They can see you clearly from every side. Thus, everything is strongly manifested. You can hide things somewhere else, but when you get home, you allow yourself to manifest things that you normally hold under the lid at work and other places. It is precisely this closeness that creates the sharpness of these relationships.

— *There is also fear here. One is afraid to hurt the people one loves.*

— Exactly. When you see a human being who suffers and consider yourself to be the cause of his suffering, you hurt even more.

— *Relationships with people who are close to us are difficult because we all want to be comfortable at home, and since each one of us pursues his own aims and defines comfort differently, we start to see a mismatch between what happens around us and what we want. As a result, we start to look for shortfalls in our surroundings. That leads to conflicts and negative states. I want to add that close people are not necessarily those who you have spent a long time with. Sometimes, you can understand people very fast, and they become close to you. It sometimes happens from day one.*

— What about such people as your mother, father, and relatives? A child gets born into a certain family. A child also choses. Actually, a child's Soul chooses the place where it wants to be born. It is not coincidental that each one of us gets born into a certain time period, at a certain place, and to certain parents. The conditions one gets born into allocate and create the best opportunities to solve the assignments one will have to solve in this incarnation. By solving these assignments, we can understand something very important. It is not easy to understand these things. Understanding comes as we go through suffering and only if we apply strong effort. That's why we need close personal relationships.

— *My relationship with my parents was very difficult until I learned that we choose our parents ourselves. I used to blame my parents for everything, but one day, I encountered the idea that a child chooses his parents himself. I suddenly thought, "Why don't I accept this idea and look at the situation from this point of view? If I chose my parents myself, I must figure out why I chose them? What kind of lessons did I decide to go through with them?" And it changed my relationship with them completely. I stopped blaming them for everything. I stopped being indignant. I stopped feeling disenchantment. Instead, I started to think and to search for solutions. I understood that if things are the way they are, it means this is necessary. I suddenly felt calm.*

Do we really choose our parents?

— We can agree or disagree with the idea that a child's Soul chooses its parents, but even if you simply try to accept this idea and work within its frame, you will see how your relationship with them will change. Instead of blaming them and pitying yourself, you will start to search for the answers. You will start to solve your assignments. You will start to understand why this situation was given to you and what you need to do there. Perhaps, it is precisely this idea that will bring a good inner state to you that will help you to solve many problems that appear during your interaction with people who are close to you. Let's say we choose our parents. How about other relatives and friends? We choose certain people consciously or subconsciously, applying efforts in order for them to be with us—husband, wife, and friends. These people usually are not forced on us, but it is precisely with these people that we experience many challenging situations. Why do we choose these people with whom we suffer later on?

"My life would have been different if I had not met you. Everything would have been totally different," you say. Blame, misunderstanding, and dead end again. But the two of you did meet. Why did you meet? What for? Why does a human being frequently find himself a wife or a husband, gets divorced, and then finds another human being with whom he repeats the same scenario? Why does this continue endlessly? Perhaps we really need to understand something in ourselves. Why do these people come into our life? What do you need to change in yourself to change your relationships with the people that are close to you?

Do you want to be right or do you want to be happy?

— *I think this is just a habit that was inculcated in us during chidhood, a certain stereotypical behavior that prevents us from behaving differently.*

— Yes, it appears that we are incapable of behaving differently. We approach a human being with a certain template. We have strict and harsh notions about what he should do and what he should not do. However, life introduces corrections and we realize that our template is incongruent with what is going on. We try to hold on to our template, but to no avail. We only receive problems and suffering as a result.

So, what kinds of problems appear in our relationships with relatives and the people who are close to us? Let's talk about things that bother you the most.

— *Every relationship can be seen as one scheme: everyone wants to be right. Every one of us wants to be right. We try to prove our rightness irrespective of anything. If I am right, I am happy. But my partner is also right. He also tries to prove himself right. Instead of trying to understand each other, we occupy ourselves with this eternal fight.*

— I want to ask these people a question: "Do you want to be right or do you want to be happy?"

— *What is hapiness? Isn't it a certain comfortable state when you understand that you are right?*

— Everyone is right in his own way. For example, a father tells his son, "You have to study and clean after yourself. You need to do this and that." It appears that he is right, but at the same time his and his son's life is horrible. When he screams at his son and insists he does this and that, he is right. However, neither one of them is happy. There is no understanding between them. Those based on *demands* conversations only lead them to separate even more. Even though they live on the same territory, they are far away from each other, and they drift further and further apart. Every one of them is right, but there is no intimacy between them. There is no unity. They separate further and further.

— I went through this myself. I see it now as two people; each is sitting in his own cocoon. They don't touch each other. Each one of them has his own life in his own cocoon, and these lives don't intersect. It seems to me, that it is precisely for this reason that misunderstanding develops. If happiness for me is mutual understanding, the opportunity to understand another human being, then perhaps it would be worthwhile to refuse the habitual point of view and to think about why another human being does what he does and to try to understand him. One needs to get out of his cocoon and to look at what is going on with another human being. One must make at least a small hole in one's cocoon; that would be a step toward another human being.

— It is interesting to look at how people appraise their relationships. Do you think we can view it as an improvement in the relationship if two human beings become closer spiritually? What contributes to the connection between people's souls? What brings them closer? What leads to their separation? We frequently use the criteria — "Who is right?" We try to prove or to force our point of view onto another human being. Yes, we might be right in our own way, but does it make us closer? Do we become more intimate, or on the contrary, drift even further apart from each other?

— In my opinion, one of the most important problems in people's interaction is that a human being always considers himself to be right. In that case, for the situation to resolve and everyone to be happy, another human being should change. I think it is very important to understand and to become aware of the fact that everything starts with me. My happiness does not start with another human being, it starts with me. It is not another human being who should change; I should change. I have the same problem myself. I frequently catch myself thinking that everything is fine with me, — "I am okay. It's you who understand that you are wrong and change something."

The rope that strangles the loved one

— Compromise can be achieved by different methods. How do cowboys catch horses? A horse is running, and a cowboy throws a lasso, catches it, and pulls the horse toward himself. Many people try to get close the same way. They throw a lasso and catch another human being. Then they tighten the knot around the victim's throat and pull it toward themselves. But that person also throws his lasso in return. Now they stand facing each other, suffocated half to death, panting from such *closeness*. Is this good? It would probably be better if two people could move freely to get close to each other. But people don't want to make these steps on their own. They want to force others to make these steps toward them. Real closeness, however, is only possible when two human beings move toward each other on their own. Two human beings walk toward each other. Someone may move slower, and someone may move faster, but if both move toward each other, they would get closer because both have this desire. If only one of them has this desire, they may never get close.

— *I like your lasso analogy. It is true, we frequently throw lassos and tie ourselves to each other and consider this to be love. Perhaps we should let each other go to understand whether we are really in love or are only dealing with an attachment.*

— Our relationships are frequently built on attachments to what we want from another human being. In the process, we tie each other with multiple ropes/desires. We are tied not only neck to neck, but arms to arms and legs to legs. Using such a mesh, we pull another human being toward ourselves. Imagine this. Would you feel good if I were to tie you up and pull you somewhere, with you being unable to move on your own? No! So, you should drop all your hang-ups and attachments first. In

117

this case, two people can at least can stand in front of each other at a comfortable distance. They can decide whether they want to turn their backs to each other or approach each other. In this case, it would be a free decision between free human beings.

Who in a family can relax?

— *I am irritated with the people who are close to me. I want to understand the reason behind this irritation and resolve it. I want my family to live peacefully. One comes home to rest and to have some peace. One has enough irritation at work. I want to see smiling, happy faces at home, but instead I am being screamed at for some minor errors, or I start to scream at them.*

— We see home as a place where we can come to relax. Why do we want to relax? We want to relax because we got very tense, irritated, and upset at work. We drag this irritation home. Our spouses also bring their problems home. Can family be a place of relaxation in this case? Each one of us needs to relax, but others can only give us what they have at the moment. And what can we give to each other except irritation, if each one of us came home in an irritated state? We need to take a deeper look at ourselves and to think about what we bring home with us. Let's say you brought a grudge home today, but for some reason you expect others to bring calmness and happiness. Others await the same from you. They also bring a lot of negativity home but for some reason expect you to bring them something good. So, first, you need to become calm and happy yourself. The question is, how?

We spoke about family, but it is impossible to separate the place we spend our entire day from the place we come to in the evening, as we transfer our irritation from one place to another. Quite frequently, family becomes a place where a human being gets even more irritated. When a few unhappy people get together on one territory, their state amplifies. If you wanted to but did not allow yourself to say something rude at work in order not to get into a conflict with your boss, you will not be able to contain yourself at home. How long can you restrain your irritation? Eventually it will spill out, usually over something trifle.

— *What if we are reasonable people? Can we come to an agreement? Can we come home from work and not interfere with each other for a couple of hours?*

— If such an opportunity really existed, it could have been a solution to your problem. But can you really agree not to scream and not to get upset with each other if everything inside you is angry and screams because of your dissatisfaction with the entire world? You come home and see a truce letter hanging on the wall. It says that no one has the right to scream, yell, or break dishes here. If you were to see this, you would run away to some other place where no such truce exists, because it is simply imperative for you to spill your state out.

— *Let's agree that people never scream without a reason. They always need a reason for that. For example, a man comes home and finds that he does not like something there. In my case, my father is deaf. I come home late at night and find him by the TV with the sound turned all the way up. I tell him I have a headache and need to rest. I even bought him a set of good headphones, but he does not care. How can I come to peace with him? We are reasonable people. I understand this, but he does not.*

— Everything would be different if relationships between people were built on reasons alone. However, they are frequently built on emotions. Can you agree, for example, to feel love and tenderness toward me at six pm today and then, at nine pm, to feel tenderness and happiness? It would be very interesting if we were to solve family problems this way. But that is not going to work, because if you are angry, you are angry. If you are discontented, you are discontented. And as most people can neither control nor manage their emotions, they get involved in multiple conflicts. A man comes home and sees a puddle of liquid on the floor. A storm follows. He starts to yell and scream. He screams about horrible things that happened in his life. He screams about his frustration with his home and his family. The visible reason is a small puddle of urine produced by his toddler, but behind it, in reality, is an enormous amount of irritation accumulated by him over the years.

It's precisely in these close personal relationships that everything gets manifested. If we don't try to change our states, we will not be able to change the climate and the emotional state of our families.

— *If there is irritation and no psychological comfort at home, it is not really a home; it is just a place to sleep, that's all.*

— If we were to take a look at a hundred different households, we would see this picture in ninety-nine of them. But nevertheless, people call these places home. They don't have any other home. They may want to find another home, but where is would they find it? So, let's think about how you can improve the home you currently have. Of course, you can run around looking for another, better home, but you are unlikely to find it in the state you are in. You must create your home yourself. When I come home in a bad mood, I introduce a certain energy into the psychological climate of my family. When I come home calm and happy, I bring in a totally different energy. Family climate is the sum of the deposits each one of its members makes. Negative deposits brought in by some of its members can be so strong that the positive deposits brought in by other family members may not be sufficient to change the overall climate. So, what does each one of us bring to the place we call home, and how does our home climate change because of it?

A family pact of nonaggression

— *I tried to come to terms with my mother and sister in order to bring calmness and tranquility to our home. I tried to get us not to scream at home and to respect each other. Based on my experience, it takes about two days for one of us to break this agreement. Initially, everyone agreed and was willing to try it, but in the end, we were either strongly attached to certain stereotypical mode of behavior or didn't have enough will power to follow with the new agreement.*

— When people start living together, they are happy and love each other, but with time they start to argue and fight with each other. Some say, "What do I need this for? Let's get a divorce." Some get a divorce, while others continue in this nightmare for a long time. Worsening physical and psychological states force them to isolate from each other. They start to avoid each other. When you look at such families, everything might appear to be quiet on the surface. No one is screaming, but not because they love each other, but because they have realized that if they are to continue in such a mode, they would kill each other. Everything is quiet, but there is no love there. There is no real relationship there, only emptiness. A human being comes home after work and enters emptiness. He comes because he is in the habit of coming to this house and being there. He is afraid to change his life. He is afraid to look for something new. He does not want to change this situation. Let's allow things to be the way they are. Let us live on our own as long as we don't interfere with each other's lives. But can such a relationship lead to unity? No, they just don't interfere with each other's existence.

— *I want to say a few words about the idea of coming to terms with each other. It seems to me, it would not be a bad idea if we were to write on the wall, "If I scream, it is not because I hate someone here, but because I feel bad." If people were to come to terms with each other, they would come to mutual understanding and start to love each other.*

— You are right. Quite frequently people scream at each other because the irritation one of them carries increases the same feeling in another human being. Perhaps, instead of mutual accusations and condemnations they should address that. They should discuss the states each one of them happens to be in, and help each other get out of these negative states. But first, they need to become aware of the states they are in. Only then they will be able to help others do the same. If your husband screams at you, he screams not because he hates you, but because he happens to be in a state he cannot get out of. In this respect, every family is akin to a team of mountain climbers where the life of each team member depends on other members of the team—they are one pack. If one falls, everyone can follow him. Therefore, it is very important to help each other get up. And if people can stand strong on their own feet in this household, in this family, if they are sure of themselves and of each other, the reason for conflicts disappears. Many conflicts resolve on their own, because as a rule, people scream, yell, and fight each other not out of strength but out of weakness, because they are unsure of themselves. So, our job is to help each other to become stronger, more confident, and independent. The alliance of two weak people is doomed to be unhappy and full of conflicts, while the alliance of two strong people can be beautiful.

What to do with irritation?

— Let's say I understand that my irritation is not connected to someone but to the fact that I am internally imbalanced. Will that understanding make life easier for the people I am living with? I doubt that. In seeing the unhappiness in me, they will experience and manifest unhappiness too. Last night my entire family was having dinner in a good mood, when suddenly my irritated son showed up. He came in and started to scream at us. We could not take this calmly.

— You will not be able to take this calmly if you are in the same state he is in. In that case, the only difference between you and him is that he manifests his feelings while you don't. A human being who clearly manifests his irritation dramatizes and reinforces the same state in people who are close to him. But **no one can force you to experience a state that is not in you.** Calmness will only come when you start to harmonize your inner world.

We have discussed this at length already. **I keep reminding you that a man who is working on the harmonization of his inner world can remain calm in any situation.** You can provide support to someone who came to you in an unbalanced state only if you do this work. You cannot calm anyone if you are not calm yourself. If you are irritated, you will get even more irritated by someone's presence. That's why you should work on your own state more and harmonize yourself.

— Let's take the example I brought up further. My son comes home and starts to scream at us. If family members understand that he is screaming at them not because he hates them, but because of his own problems, we can allow him to speak up and to become aware of his issues.

— This is a viable option, but only if you understand that his unhappiness has not been caused by you. This is a very important moment. Usually, when our family member gets irritated, we immediately think that he is irritated because of us. This is not necessarily the case. He may be unhappy because something happened in his life that he cannot understand and accept yet. If you understand that you are not responsible for what has happened to him, you can stay calm and help him to sort out what is going on in him.

— *That's great, but let me tell you what has been happening to me repeatedly. I come home with the intention of trying to be aware of myself. My mom comes to the living room, sees me in a great mood, and says, "You went out this morning without cleaning the mess you have made on the kitchen table. You have not washed the dishes." I came home in a great mood, and I hear that. I understand that those are her problems, but her statement hits me hard. I know that I have not done what I was supposed to do. I cannot be detached anymore. I get upset.*

— You have positioned yourself very interestingly. This is not your mom's problem. This is a problem which both of you share. You probably would not want to live in this house if it was filled with garbage.

— *I understand that, but I have caused my mom irritation only because she felt bad. I, on the other hand, felt good. Is that right? Let's turn it around. I come home angry, irritated, and ready to kill everyone. I tell her that I cannot finish the work I started last month. She tells me that I am an idiot; I should not have started what I cannot finish. But at the same time, she feeds me dinner and tries to take my mind off my problems by discussing the latest movie she has seen... I feel like I was spanked and then was gently kissed on the cheek. It is not easy to refuse that.*

"I feel bad because you feel good…"

— Exactly. Quite frequently one of us feels good, while another feels bad. All of us have experienced these situations.

— *I would like to review a similar situation. It seems to me that the main reason people living together are unhappy is because their desires and moods do not coincide in time, even though, in general, they want the same thing. They may have the same habits and interests, but at the moment, one of them may want to be by himself while his partner wants company. So, when one of them manifests his state, the other does not respond to it. That leads to disharmony. I don't know what to do with this.*

— Do you respect your partner's rights to have his or her own individual states or inner experience? How often do these rights get broken in your family? Are they being accepted at all?

— *An interesting situation developed in my family where I have to help to regulate the relationship between my parents. My mom is incapable of either manifesting her desires or doing something on her own. That bothers me, not only because I must stand between them, but also because I see my mother in myself. I feel her in me, and that scares me. I don't even know how to help them. When they are in a good mood, everything is great, but when they are in a bad mood, something terrible happens. Even when they don't fight, they are frequently not on speaking terms with each other. A tremendous stress is experienced by everyone in the house. Mom is being killed by that. My dad appears to be the oppressor. I don't know what to do in these situations since both of them are in me.*

— When parents try to regulate their conflicts, they frequently use their children as buffers. If they are not on speaking terms at the moment, they may start to communicate through a child, spilling everything they did not spill onto each other onto the child. This traumatizes the child.

— *Moreover, each one of them tries to pull the child to his side. They lasso the kid from both sides and suffocate him.*

— The main reason this happens is that neither one of them wants to take responsibility for what is happening. Both try to correct the situation by manipulating each other, and because neither one of them wants that to happen, the child is used as a bargaining chip. This manipulation through a child leads to the escalation of drama in the family, and increases the split in the child's psyche. That leads to a malfunction in his inner world, as the child carries inside him the father, the mother, and other close people. They are all in him. If parental conflict has not been solved by the parents, it will be transferred to the inner world of a child, who will suffer while trying to solve it throughout his lifetime. Parents transmit their problems to their children, problems that later determine their life and fate. If they were incapable of solving them on their own, they leave it to their children. Until one family member is ready to accept the responsibility for everything that happens in the family and starts to solve these problems independently, inside himself, the situation will continue to go from bad to worse.

If one member of the family accepts this responsibility and says to himself, "What happens in our family is the result of our mutual unwillingness to change ourselves. I am ready to do this, and I will do it irrespective of whether other members of my family are ready for it or not." If such a human being shows up in a family, he can do a lot for everybody.

When asked to take responsibility, most people say, "Why should I do it when others don't want to do anything? I have done a lot already, but no one helps me." What can you say to him? We can only say one thing: "The one who starts to do it will succeed. If you stop doing that, things will only get

126

worse." In this business, you can only depend on yourself. If you have come to conclusion that old relationships are unsustainable and you don't want things to continue the way they are, you must start changing the situation inside yourself. These people are next to you for a reason. You need them to see yourself. The conditions you are currently in are the best conditions for you. Perhaps these conditions are very difficult, but these are the best conditions for your self-understanding. When you find the way to use them correctly, everything around you will start to change. Your changes will lead to changes in those who are next to you. Irritation is contagious. However, calmness, self-assuredness, and a desire to resolve the situation can be equally contagious. When you start to cultivate and strengthen your stillness, those who surround you will feel it. They will start to change too. Perhaps, this will not happen fast, but this will happen.

— *I wanted to mention two cocoons in which family members live. I think that if one family member were to try to understand the interests of those with whom he lives, everything will change.*

— *My family lives in a state of irritation. Mom comes home from work and brings aggression. She tells me, "It's your fault. You are the guilty one." I take it without fighting, and dad is quiet too. I can only recall one quarrel when they really got mad at each other.*

— We are going to discuss the energy interaction that occurs when people live in close proximity to each other. Certain parts of these people activate each other strongly. In essence, a human being is an energy unit. As people interact, their energies start to come into contact. This process occurs intensely in a family. For example, when a human being screams, a strong wave of low-vibrational energy spreads from him. If a similar wave of energy moves toward him, it results in an explosion. One human being should remain silent for a period of time, otherwise, there is going to be an explosion. He becomes silent, but what boils inside him does not disappear. On the contrary, it gets stronger. Eventually, he finds a moment when the one who screamed at him gets energetically weak, and he starts to yell at him or her. That's what happens on the energy level.

— *In a family unit, irritation is frequently spilled onto a child. Parents can bring up a child to be a loser in order to dump their irritation on him and have someone to blame. That's what happened in my family. As soon as enough irritation would get accumulated, it would be spilled onto me.*

The "beloved" child or a "scapegoat"?

— Yes, some parents make a lightning rod out of a child to ground their negative emotions. They need this lightning rod and they take care of it and make sure it functions well. When such a child gets weak and starts to fall, they try to dump their anger somewhere else. Perhaps what I say sounds horrible to you. You may say, "No, this is not my family." You might not have done this consciously, but subconsciously you might have done precisely that. As the weakest member of a family, a child can easily be turned into a scapegoat. People tend to find scapegoats and dump their negative emotions onto them. When one such a scapegoat dies, they find another one, because they cannot live without one. It is usually a child who takes this role in a family, but it could be someone else. It becomes his or her professional responsibility. The life of such children is horrible; a tremendous amount of negative energy passes through them. Imagine you grabbed a hot wire, and a high voltage passes through you. That's what such children feel. Do people who pass their irritation through their kids ever think about what they feel? Such children usually burn out fast. So, everything is not as simple as it appears, but it does not mean that we can't change it.

First, we need to understand what really happens, and then, we need to start to change things. We need to harmonize our relationships with other people. The more flexible our relationships with people are, the more harmonious our relationships with them are going to be. We should all think about whether we should conduct the current of our irritation through a human being who is next to us or not. Most frequently, when people come to such a state, they don't think of anything anymore. They just want to dump and unload what they have accumulated. They unload it onto the first person they encounter, and they usually use someone close to them as a lightning rod. Later, this human being will use the same strategy in his relationships with other people. A vicious circle appears, and if we don't become aware of it, it will continue indefinitely.

When you start to understand what is happening with you and around you, you will be able to observe and to become aware of what is really happening. When you start to do something in a state of awareness, things start to change. Try screaming while being aware of yourself screaming. I can tell you that soon things will start to change around you. You will suddenly get into a totally different state just because you become aware of what you are doing. Have you tried to be aware of yourself while interacting with other people?

— *I experienced that this morning. I did not scream at anyone. I was doing something very specific. Someone distracted me. My first reaction was habitual; I almost screamed at him. But suddenly, I realized that no one will benefit from my screaming. I don't know to where exactly this energy was transformed, but I suddenly felt good. I felt calm and comfortable. I understood that I did not have to scream at anyone.*

— This is a very important question. Most people go through life without any awareness of themselves. When they feel irritation, they simply dump it onto the people around them. Tell them that unawareness has severe negative consequences for them and those around them, and most of them will reply, "I don't care. I will do what I want to do anyway." In this case, what happened to them will continue to happen, but their lessons will become heavier and heavier. Another man will say, "I agree with you. I will start to observe what happens to me and around me. I can see how my aggression and the anger I dump on people returns to me. I am not satisfied with this state of affairs. I understand this, but what can I do? I have tried to fight this anger of mine, but I didn't get anywhere."

So, I will tell you again, "You don't need to fight anything. You just need to observe your anger." The first thing you need to understand is that your negative outbursts don't lead anywhere. They misbalance you. Moreover, they misbalance the people next to you. The second step is to start to observe your feelings, thoughts, and actions. You arrive at the irritated state without awareness. You can start to observe and to become aware of your states: "Yes, I am in an irritated state right now." In doing that, you can say to your partner, "You know, I am in a very irritated state right now. You probably feel that. I have been dealing with a serious problem at work and I am unable to get rid of the memories associated with it. I came home in a very irritated state. Let's just sit down and talk. I am in such a state right now that I simply don't know what to do." If you say that, your partner will relate to you in a different way. He or she may say, "Yes, I know how it is. I was in a similar state yesterday. I understand you." If, on another hand, you arrive home in an irritated state without explaining anything, he might think that you are irritated with him. That will get him irritated too. It is enough just to say that your state has nothing to do with him and to acknowledge that you want to be free of this state. Simply verbalizing this fact will allow you to change your state. We need to go deeper. We need to observe what we say, how we say it, and to whom we say what we say all the time. You will not be able to get rid of irritation right away. Based on inertia, it will continue for a certain period of time. Just observe it. It will change as you become increasingly aware of yourself.

— *What if another human being perceives my words about my irritation as manipulation?*

— Yes, that can happen. But if you are honest, you will find understanding on the other end. He will understand that you are not trying to manipulate him, but are really trying to change something in yourself. Our habitual relationships are very inert. This inertia manifests itself especially strongly in families. When people have been relating to each other in a certain way for years, they cannot transform right away. Therefore, the moment you become aware of the situation as a dead end and realize that things cannot go on the way they used to be is very important. The habitual stereotypes don't lead us anywhere; changing them is not easy either. Changes are painful, but to build new, harmonious relationships, you must allow them to occur.

Everything, whether good or bad, has its inertia. For example, you may have old friends with whom you have spent your childhood playing. Life moved you apart and you live in different cities now. You meet twenty years later, and you find yourself in a warm, friendly relationship again. This is the inertia of good relationships.

— *I want to comment on the relationship of Andrey and his mother. When he comes home in a good mood, she reprimands him on the things he has not done around the house. When he comes home tired, she does something to uplift his mood. I think his mom manipulates him very well. It is not coincidental that he speaks about manipulation all the time. It looks like he was exposed to manipulation since childhood. Looks like she has not realized herself, and she tries to do it through him now. When she sees him unhappy, she thinks, "I am going to support him today. I will make him feel good." But when he comes home in a good mood, she thinks, "I supported him yesterday. Let's get to work now. Let me do what I need to do with him now." She doesn't know how to do it differently.*

— In essence, she reacts to herself through him. When she sees her son, i.e. herself, angry, she calms him down. When she sees him, i.e. herself, in a happy state, she does something to move him to a different state. That's the way she relates to herself. That's why we say that the world is a mirror, and the people who are close to us are big mirrors that reflect us and our relationship with ourselves. When we try to change our friends and relatives, we move further away from our basic assignment, which is to change ourselves. We can clearly see how we relate to ourselves and what dissatisfies us about ourselves through our relatives and friends. Our task is very clear. We must change ourselves in order to relate to another human being the way we relate to ourselves. This principle was known to early Christians, but how many people realize it? We need to relate to other people the way we relate to ourselves. At the same time, we need to love ourselves, because if we don't love ourselves, we will relate to others the same way we relate to ourselves—with accusation and blame.

— I want to explain how I see this situation. Mom took a lot on her shoulders, and she got used to that. When she says, "You have not made your bed. You have not washed the dishes. You have not taken the trash out," she understands that if I don't do it, she will have to do it herself. Perhaps she does not want to do that, but she does it anyway. She accepts this responsibility, and she will continue to do that. Perhaps it is Mom who should try not to do that?

— This is a great question that deals with the chores family members perform around the house. Frequently, people organize their daily communication around these chores. They can spend hours discussing who is going to do the dishes. At the end of a day, a sink full of dirty dishes is not the worst thing that can happen to a family. The awful relationships between people, which appear because of constant fighting about who is going to do what around the house, is much worse. What is more important to you: the cleanliness of the dishes or the cleanliness of your relationships?

— It looks like family relationships are manipulatory in nature. We try to manipulate others to force them to do what we want them to do. For example, I adopted my mom's mode of behavior a long time ago. I have done it without any awareness. When someone feels good, I try to hit him as hard as I can.

"I will never be the way my parents are!"

— What is behind this common parent/child conflict? At a certain age, a child tells his parents, "I will never be the way Dad is! I will never be the way my mom is!" Time passes. A child grows up, gets married, establishes his own family, gives birth to his own children, and becomes a copy of his parents. That happens all the time and continues until this grown-up child becomes aware of his relationships with his parents, even if they live in another country or have passed away. The parents are inside this child, who is now a grown-up adult. Whatever was going on in the family when the child was growing up is in him now.

— *The more I listen to you, the more I realize how strongly I resemble my mother. I perceive other people as something incomplete, as something I need to work on and finish. They need to be given a good lesson in the form of a kick or a slap. If they are hurting afterwards, they must be supported.*

— **That's why it is so important to come to love your parents**. This kind of relationship to parents is fixed in many traditions as a style of relationships. Can you come to love and understand God and the Earth on which we live if you don't love your parents? Can you even love someone if you don't love and don't understand your father and mother? Parents are Gods to a child. They are big creatures who know everything. Later, a child may realize that they don't know much, but that's what he thinks when he is little. Every child relates to his parents as if they were all knowing gods leading him on his life journey. A man who is unable to love his parents will not be able to love anyone else. He will transfer his conflicts with his parents onto his future partners. Why did the idea of God as a reprimanding, appraising, judging, and punishing for every mistake father get so widely accepted here? If you do something bad, he punishes you. If you do something good, he praises you. This is just a projection of common family relationships. Most people don't know anything else.

It is extremely important to come to love and understand your parents from the point of view of spiritual development.

— *So, what is the most important thing in a family: the aims family members pursue or the people themselves? As a rule, dissatisfaction appears inside a family because different members pursue different goals. I*

134

encountered a situation a few weeks ago, when I had to manipulate my own parents. I looked at them as the figurines on a chess board.

— A child learns how people relate to each other while growing up in a family. Later, he transfers these relationships onto other people and onto the world at large. If family members manipulate each other, a child will never believe that other types of relationships exist. If this child grows up to be a politician or gets into a position of power, he will start to realize a habitual for him style of relationships. Therefore, it is very important to understand why people unite, what unites them, and what their aims are. Is there something that unites all of us, one aim that can unite all of us—parents, children, nations, and countries?

— *When I get together with my old friends and have a drink, we recall good old times, when we had a common aim and common interests. We don't have them anymore. The only thing we do is reminisce. I wish we had a common aim.*

— What is an aim? One aim separates people and leads to a conflict. Another unites them and leads to unity. It is important to understand the aims you set up for yourself. Why do you unite? Why do you want to create a family?

"I want to get married!" — "Why?"

— *Marriage is just a ritual. People get in a car, drive to the local City Hall, and put rings on each other's fingers. That's it. Many of them, including me, get a divorce a few years later.*

— What do people look for in a marriage? You meet someone, and you decide to be together. Do you really need to go to City Hall, get a ring on your finger, and be called husband and wife to be together? Perhaps you don't need that.

But you wanted to be together. Why did you decide to split? What united you when you met, and why did you separate?

— *I couldn't accept what I did not like in her. I could not do anything about it.*

— There was something you did not like in her.

— *Yes. Moreover, I did not want to do anything about it, or maybe I wanted to do something but was not strong enough ... I don't know.*

— What did you expect from that relationship? What was the impulse behind it? Many people divorce. This is common nowadays. Many people know that family life is not all sugar and roses, but people get together nevertheless. So, there must be an impulse that forces people to do that. What is it?

— *Most likely it is a need to come home and to have a shoulder to lean on, to cry on if you need to.*

— So, it's a place where you can relax. It's a place where someone will understand, comfort, and perhaps console you.

— *Yes.*

— Does anyone else want to share with us what influenced him to unite his life with another human being?

— *I dont think it really matters whether people are legally married or not, but this legal document carries some kind of responsibility. I think when people live together without being officially married, it is easier for them to split.*

— This piece of paper is just a formality for you, but this formality can influence you quite significantly if your parents don't see it as formality. They could tell you that this is inappropriate and not how people do things. It might be a serious mater. If your parents or relatives consider this ceremony to be important, they might try to influence you. Do you think you need to make your relationship more formal by signing a marriage license?

— *No, I don't need to do that.*

— But what does a relationship not formalized by a marriage license offer to people? Does it offer an easier way to separate? Does it offer a freer relationship with less strings attached?

How to build your "cell of society" better

— *I think this formality is necessary for people to live more comfortably in society.*

— Do you think two human beings should accept some kind of responsibility for each other when they start to live together? Is this necessary? This responsibility may vary. Some people may go to City Hall and do what most people do, i.e. reinforce their relationship by signing a legal marriage contract and by putting rings on each other's fingers. Others may have an informal agreement. Should two people living together be responsible for each other in close relationships, or is this totally unnecessary?

— *I think it is better if two people can agree between themselves without any legal documents.*

— What should they agree on? Should they agree to come to a certain place at a certain time every day and to call this place home?

— *They can agree to respect each other's desires and to accept each other the way they are.*

— Perhaps this is not necesary. Perhaps love is something you feel today and don't feel tomorrow. What kind of agreements can there be in that case? Feelings change. Or is it different in your case? Perhaps you think, "I know I need to get married. I know children get born when people start to sleep together, and, therefore, I need to make this relationship formal." In that case, you need an agreement. Do we take responsibility for what we do, for the children we may give birth to, and for many other things, or is it all only about feelings and emotions: today I feel like being with you, but I don't know what is going to happen tomorrow? I can't promise you anything.

— *I wanted to say something about this marriage license. There is a common notion that is quite prevalent nowadays that you can live the way you want and do anything you want with your life. It's your life. You can see whoever you want, whether you are married or not, but for some reason, if you want to have kids, you should get married. I don't remember anyone telling me this, but this is in me: my child is going to be raised in society, and I should create the necessary conditions for him to be normally adapted to society.*

— What does the phrase "normally adapted to a society" mean? What is important to you? Is it important to you that your child can say that he is not a bastard, that he has mom and dad, and that he was born in wedlock, or are you talking about something deep and connected to the feeling of a child who is growing in a family where ether mom or dad is absent? Do you think this situation, where one parent is absent, leaves a mark on a child?

— *Many of my friends came from broken families; most of them where brought up without a father figure. At one point, I even conducted an investigation, trying to figure out whether some kind of sexual attraction between mothers and sons exist in such families. Many boys run away from homes because of this. They frequently hear from their mothers, "I fed you and I took care of you. I worked two jobs to bring you up." These boys must deal with many problems later. Some of them become homosexuals.*

Where parental "insufficiency" leads

— Well, let's not bring sexual orientation into this just yet, but this is quite an important topic. The way I see it, when a single mother brings up a child, she concentrates on him to a significant degree. She gets overly attached to him. If she had a husband, she would spend some of her energy on him, and in that case, her relationships with her children would have been different. But in this case, a certain insufficiency or deficiency develops.

Such an insufficiency develops when one of the parents is absent from a family. A child gets born out of the union of two people, whether they have been together for one hour or five years. Both masculine and feminine parts are present in every child. There is a masculine part in every woman and a feminine part in every man, and when one of the parents is absent during childhood, a child gets deprived in terms of the development of the corresponding part. Have you noticed that? For example, a girl who was brought up by mother alone may develop difficulties in her relationships with men, because her father was absent when she was growing up, and she did not receive the masculine energy that would have strengthened her masculine side.

— *I am such a girl. I was brought up by my mom without a father. I totally agree with you. A total concentration on a child leads to the child's desire to run away. I felt Dad's absence every minute of my life. First it was unconscious, but later, I became aware of it. However, I have carried something positive out of this situation too. In respect to my relationships with men, I think Dad's absence played a positive role for me. In my case, Mom's attitude toward men was not transferred to me. There were no men in my family when I was growing up.*

— But you must have heard conversations about men. Are you telling us you don't know how your mom related to them?

— *I know how she related to men, but her attitude did not transfer to me. My relationship to men is totally different, because...*

— Perhaps it is the same in your case, but reversed?

— *That might be true.*

— And you are telling us it was not transferred to you? This is impossible. Everything instilled in you during childhood will have consequences. You may develop an attitude which is opposite to your mom's attitude, but you must lean on what you have experienced, nevertheless. You either take what Mom had, or you take the side opposite to hers.

— *Perhaps her experience taught me how not to relate to men. I relate to men differently, and my relationships with them make me happy.*

— Who else wants to share his or her experience of growing up in a single parent household?

A man and a woman inside you

— *For some reason, I performed a masculine role from early childhood. Mom saw a man in me, and during adolescence, I did everything a man does in a household. Thus, I feel my masculine side more than I probably should. I experience serious problems in my relationships with men because of it.*

— Everything in this world represents the interaction of two interrelated energies. The Chinese call them *Yin* and *Yang*. Everything in this world is created through their interaction. If we were to take what is called Spirit, for example, God, or Supreme Aspect — this is masculine energy. The Earth is feminine energy. A human being and humanity at large are born out of the interaction between masculine and feminine principles. Harmonization is possible only when the correct interaction between these energies is present. You have probably seen the symbol for Yin and Yang, where black and white colors give birth to each other and wash each other as two friendly hands. There are no superiors and no inferiors there. It's an interaction of two equal energies.

Each human being should realize this principle. That will bring happiness and harmony into our lives. A human being is born of a man and a woman. He has both masculine and feminine origins. When one of them starts to prevail in detriment to the other, an imbalance appears that manifests itself in multiple problems. The breakdown of principles of interaction between masculine and feminine energies leads to distortions, which manifest themselves within the family. When the masculine or feminine origin is significantly reduced, or, on the contrary, when one of the origins prevails in a child, the movement of energy in a child's structure becomes disharmonious. Someone needs to reinforce his masculine side, while someone else must reinforce his or her feminine side to harmonize the interrelationships of these energies in themselves. Some people develop within their family a dislike toward men—they cannot accept their fathers. Others don't accept their mothers. Some cannot accept either parent. Many such people suffer because of this imbalance their entire lives. Everything that happens to them is a result of the father/mother conflict that continues inside them. It is imperative to understand that, as you will not be able to love yourself until you start to love your parents. You will not be able to throw them out of yourself. No one can do this. You can separate physically by moving to another country, but you will not be able to throw them out of your system. We must learn to love our parents inside ourselves. It might be difficult, but it is possible. We will not be able to do anything until we do that.

— *We have to understand that our parents were someone else's children once. They were roasted and scoffed by their parents the same way our parents later roasted and scoffed us. The word "scoffed" came out of my mouth involuntary, but that's how it frequently is. All of us are victims of our childhood upbringing. Our parents are similar victims, and their parents…*

— How long are we going to continue to be the victims? As long as we consider ourselves to be the victims, we will not be able to change anything. The only way to accept our parents inside ourselves is to become aware of our old programs of thoughts, feelings, and actions. We must start loving them. We must find a place for them inside ourselves.

— *Can we come to love them by asking our mind and our feelings for help?*

— The mind does not love. Only the heart can love. The mind may find virtues or deficiencies. It can analyze and separate. It cannot love anyone. It is only your heart that can start to love. The heart is synthesis; it integrates everything. It unites things that the mind sees as something that can never be connected. Your mind cannot unite your parents. If you use your mind to approach your relatives, you will find as many virtues in them as you will find shortcomings. You will always be perplexed. How can I love him if he has so many shortcomings? The heart does not look at things from that point of view; it just loves. It accepts everything and everyone.

— *So, how is one to observe all of this?*

— Every human being consists of three worlds. It's really one world, but it consists of three different worlds. The world of a human being is the world of thoughts, feelings, and actions. What unites people? Why do they want to be close to each other? Why do they want to unite? Perhaps their bodies are attracted to each other, or their minds find some common ground to play on, or their hearts beat in unison.

Love–Hate

— I would like to expand on what I just said. When I speak about the heart, I speak of the "deep heart." I speak not of the physical heart, but of the spiritual center of a human being. The physical heart can be influenced by many external signals; today it likes something, and tomorrow it likes something else. I love you today, and I hate you tomorrow. The physical heart is as contradictory as the mind. When I speak of the heart, I speak of the deep, spiritual heart. When you get to that place, all people become one for you. We start to experience love for everyone, not for just one particular human being. Perhaps what I am discussing is unclear to you, but I cannot explain it in words. It can only be felt. When you start to go deep inside yourself, eventually you will come to the place where your spiritual heart is and you will feel true love. Usually, when we speak of our feelings, we touch precisely those contradictions that we harbor in our physical hearts. Love—don't love. Want—don't want. Like—don't like.

— *Does it mean one has to turn off one's mind?*

— The mind and thoughts are not emotional. The mind determines what is profitable for it. You have said that the happiest marriage is an arranged marriage that is based on calculation, but this is not the happiness you may experience if you happen to be in the area of the spiritual heart. Yes, an arranged marriage might be a convenient, quiet, and comfortable marriage in terms of the benefits it can offer to two human beings living together. You satisfy your needs

143

connected to material things, sex, and safety. You satisfy your needs connected to the necessity of having a family and children. There are many benefits in such a marriage, but it lacks true love.

Why do you get together anyway? Perhaps you get together to be comfortable. In this case, that's what you get. Most people search for love without any understanding of what love is. They find someone, and they tell him, "I love you very much." A few days later they scream at each other, "I hate you!" They just spoke of love yesterday. The physical heart is capricious, inconsistent, and dual. If we were to talk about the relationship between two people at the level of the mind, it is like a business relationship when two human beings unite to create a firm. They have a certain aim, and they perform the necessary functions to achieve it. Both are satisfied. But when a man and a woman unite based on inner attraction, the feelings they have for each other are of utmost importance. That's where all the problems that we have discussed appear.

— *Is that what we call the attachment of the heart?*

— Yes, but it is precisely what people call the attachment of the heart that later creates huge problems for them. What is the depth of your feelings? On the surface, everything is very volatile. But the deeper you go inside yourself, into the depth of your heart, the closer you get to what is unchangeable and eternal. You start to feel what unites you with other people. But you can only enter this depth of the heart when you solve all the problems that lie on the surface, i.e. in the physical heart. It is in the physical heart where the pain of unsolved problems in your relationships with the people who are close to you happens to be.

Why are so many people afraid to go deep into their heart? They are afraid because they meet their unsolved problems on the way: hatred toward their mother, disrespect and dislike of their father, etc. You will not exit this vicious circle, and you will not reach your spiritual heart unless you see and pass though these problems.

We can love our father, our mother, our sister, brother, husband, wife only to the extent that we can accept them. But what do we have now? How do we relate to them? If we can't see how we relate to them now, we will not be able to change our relationship with them. If you find these relationships to be difficult, you will not want to think about them. You will not want to return to them. But you will not be able to move further on this path unless you return and resolve them. Until you do that, these unsolved problems will run your life.

— *The heart also has memory. We forget things that brought us pain; they get duller over time. It seems to us that something has disappeared, but this is not the case. Everything is there. We just don't want to touch what is there, especially things that hurt us.*

— Yes, the heart remembers everything. It remembers every disenchantment and every grudge. But it is precisely by becoming aware of this pain that we can come to see the most important things of our life. By returning to the sufferings of our heart, re-experiencing them in a state of awareness, we exit the borders of pain and cleanse our hearts from it forever. I will ask you to become aware of what is inside your heart now. Recall what happened to you during childhood. Recall your relationship with your parents.

— *I can't force myself to love my parents. I pity them. I hate and despise them. I cannot force myself to love them. Should I force myself?*

Pain is the result of misunderstanding

— You cannot force yourself to love anyone. I am not asking you to do that. I am talking about something totally different. I am asking you to feel them and to feel what they experience toward you. The reason they caused you to experience pain, and perhaps continue to cause you to experience it, is the result of their misunderstanding. They do it because they don't understand. When they don't understand, they create pain for themselves and for you. When parents inflict pain on their children, they don't do it out of malice; they do it out of misunderstanding. Their parents did it to them, and now they do it to their children. This is done without awareness.

— *No, he understands everything. He tells me that face to face. I speak to him about it from time to time, even though it is very difficult. Afterwards, he usually slams the door and goes for a drink. He tells me, "Why should I treat you differently? That's how my parents treated me, and that's how I will treat you." He is 73 years old. I tell him, "Didn't you come to understand anything during your life?"*

— Look, you are saying the same thing to him, "You should." Why do you think he should do anything? You cannot force True Understanding on anyone. You have said that when you get into a conversation like this, he reaches for a drink. He does not go for a drink because he is happy. This situation causes him to have as much pain as it causes you. He just does not see the new opportunities and, as a result, insists on the old, habitual way of dealing with the situation. But it does not lead anywhere, and it does not make him happy.

— *He is not looking for anything new. He doesn't try to become aware of his life.*

— This is not his fault. This is his misfortune.

— I disagree. I consider it to be his fault. He got married because he was completely irresponsible, and he gave birth to children he does not even know.

— You will never be able to love him if you continue to think that this is his fault.

— Why? Since when is responsibility considered to be a fault?

— This is his misfortune, not his fault. A human being who understands that irresponsibility cannot lead to anything good will not remain irresponsible; he will accept the responsibility. If he has not done so, it means he still does not understand how awful it is, first of all, for himself. Many people are lost and make mistakes. Your father is one of them. He acts out of his best intentions, and if that does not lead to good results, it is because he is mistaken. He does not understand. He is not trying to hurt you. He does not understand what he does. And if you can see something better from your side, you should not blame him. You should try to help him understand that.

— How can I help him if he declines my help?

— You continue to blame him. You will stop that when you come to understand him, and yourself through him.

— I understand why he drinks.

— I do not hear understanding in your voice. I only hear a grudge.

— No, I really understand why he drinks, but I cannot help him.

— You can't or you don't want to?

— How can I help? I can't find him a wife.

— You can't do that. However, you can help him understand that the ways he has explored in trying to get out of his inner conflict, which as assigned to him by his parents and now transferred through him to you, lead to a dead end. **Everything here is so entangled that we will never be able**

to get out of this mess if we continue to blame. We will continue to pound our heads against the wall, increasing our irritation and hatred toward the people who are close to us. That's what is going to happen unless we start on the way that leads out of this nightmare, and the only way out of this mess is to start to understand yourself through other people. Once you start to understand other people, you will start to understand yourself, because their problems are your problems. The problems of our parents are our problems, and if we don't want to understand them, we don't want to understand ourselves. If we don't want to understand ourselves, we cannot change anything in ourselves or in our lives.

Our relatives and the people who are close to us are given to us so we can start to understand and love ourselves. When we understand them, we will understand ourselves. That will change their attitude toward us. It cannot be done by force or manipulation. It can only be done through a sincere feeling that appears in us. They have not found this feeling yet, and when we find it, they will see it too. Why does someone scream, drink, and fight? He does it because he has not found a better way out of his inner conflict. When he finds a man, who found an exit out of a similar situation, he will listen to him. We are all in similar situations, submerged in a sleep and misunderstanding of ourselves, with slightly different variations. When a human being is in a small, dark space, he runs around like crazy. He hits his head on the walls and breaks everything around him because he cannot see anything. But when he starts to see the light, he stops doing what he was doing and starts to walk toward this light. Even though this light is weak and can barely be seen, he knows the direction now. When a human being does not see anything around himself, he just runs around bumping into the walls, hurting himself and other people. Until the light of awareness appears in someone who is close to us, we don't know what to do, but when one of us develops the light of the heart, people around us get the opportunity to understand where the exit out of the dead end lies.

"One day, I understood him"

— *I would like to use myself as an example of what you have just discussed. I was in a similar situation with my dad, but one day I understood him. I came home, and he started to scream at me without any reason. I felt so bad, that I had to hide in my room. I spent some time there trying to understand what was going on. Finally, anger left me, and I felt love toward him. A few minutes later, he knocked on my door, trying to add something to what he said, but my reaction to him with was totally different than what he expected. He was surprised. He gave me a very curious glance and left. I am happy I could achieve that.*

— Yes, this is possible. Look, when one human being changes, another cannot continue to do what he did before. Perhaps when he entered your room and saw you in a different state, he understood something.

— *I grew up without a father. My mom raised me and my brother by herself. My brother got married young and moved out. I was left with Mom, who spent a lot of time with me. We got very attached to each other. At some point, I started to suffocate. I wanted freedom. I did not want her to ask me where I was, what I did, and at what time I am going to be home. I wanted to leave my clothes where I wanted to leave them, and if I wanted them on the floor, I wanted to be able to have them on the floor. I wanted to have some minimal freedom, and when I did not get it, I left home. Over the past six years, I've been in and out of the house. Our relationship was strained. I would come back home and we would live quietly for a month or two. Then we would start to fight again, and I would have to leave. We would get on each other nerves fast. She would frequently get sick, but I didn't care. I thought this was her way to manipulate me to bring me home. Finally, I started to understand her. It was very difficult for her too. She was attached to me her entire life, when suddenly I, who she considered to be her private property, left. As I started to change, our relationship started to get better. First, I started to understand myself. I understood why I left and what I wanted. I understood Mom later. I was the only one she could lean on. I was her only connection to the outside world. My brother was busy with his own family. He was not in the picture for a long time. She never remarried. I was the only one she had an emotional connection with, but this bond became pathological and difficult to break. To break this connection was to break everything. As I started to understand myself better, I started to understand her. We still don't see everything eye to eye, but I agree with her more. Right now, I am living with her. I still have to report to her where I go and when I am going to be home, but I feel better. I don't mind it anymore. We talk about things, but she does not nag me about every tiny detail all the time, and I don't bother her. I may get irritated by her behavior occasionally, but I try not to show it. I am calm. I feel better because I understand myself and her better. I was angry before. Sometimes I was so angry I couldn't speak to her on the phone. I blamed her for getting me attached to her so strongly. Now I understand some of her problems better. I can't say I understand all of them, but the more I understand and accept myself, the more I understand and accept her.*

— Why are we born here? Some of us think we are born here to change something in ourselves. Afterwards, it will be very difficult and perhaps impossible to change. We don't disappear with the death of the physical body. You can change yourself while you are in the body, but afterwards you will not be able to do that. When you get There, your unsolved problems will remain with you. You can only solve these problems here, while in the physical body. Those of you who still carry condemnation and grudges need to sort out why these feelings appeared and transform them. Do it here and now. It is precisely here and now that we have the opportunity to do it. Kathy told us about her mother who, like any other human being, wants to be loved and understood. But many people want one human being, a son or a daughter sometimes, to satisfy all their desires. They don't know how to love everyone and everything, and thus, they concentrate on their children alone. When this narrowly concentrated feeling starts to break, it causes both of you to experience pain. But at the same time, it is impossible to improve a state of this human being unless you offer him an opportunity to understand that closeness, warmth, and love can come to him from every side, not only from you. Many people become focused on one thing only. They are unable to understand that the whole world is overflowing with love; it is everywhere. And when a child leaves his parents and comes to understand that, he returns to them as a changed human being. He can now help them to expand their understanding and feeling of love.

"I left home six years ago…"

— *I left home six years ago, and I have been on my own ever since. That has allowed me to accumulate a certain experience in respect to what kind of relationships human beings, including friends and relatives, can have. I was able to look at my previous life from the side and to see what they ask of me and what I ask from them. I understood that many of my desires don't lead anywhere.*

— By leaving a habitual environment, a human being gets to know the world in its other manifestations. A child, who grows up in a family, believes that everything in the world happens the way it happens in his family, but later he starts to see and feel something else. A child develops a desire to separate and find out what's going on out there. He leaves home to explore the world. He may return later, but he will return a different human being, and he will bring to his parents his new understanding of the world. The fact that his parents are older than him does not mean they understand more. Quite frequently, this is not the case, and children can teach their parents something new. This means that not only do parents bear a responsibility for their child, but that the child bears a responsibility for his parents too. I am talking about the responsibility for understanding life the way it really is.

— *When I was young, beautiful seventeen-year old girl I was hit by a truck. I spent six months in a hospital. At first, I did not feel the consequences of this trauma, but later I realized that my psyche and body were irreparably damaged.*

My first romantic experience ended with me getting married right after high school. I soon realized that I had made a mistake, but it took me a long time to separate from my husband. It was a difficult divorce. My husband was against it. He probably loved me. He still insists I was the only love of his life. Perhaps that's true. Anyway, I tried to break this very strong bond. We used to see each other after the divorce. I have not been with another man for ten years. Later, I understood that I needed to live a full life in the name of my child. My child was growing. I observed her development and enjoyed every minute with her. It was very interesting. I don't understand those mothers who say that if the father is absent, the mother gets very attached to her child. Quite frequently nowadays, a young woman drops her child on her parents' laps. She is young and healthy. She needs a man, and a child is just a problem for her. So, she dumps her kid onto the grandparents. I, on the other hand, became fixated on my kid. I had a difficult time dealing with men. That was probably because of my difficult and demanding personality. In the end, I brought up my daughter to be my friend, and it appeared to me she was the only one who understood me well. She used to tell me, "Mom, you are the only human being in the whole world who loves me." But the time came when she turned seventeen. She decided to move out of the house. Initially, I took it well: a girl grows up and wants to have her freedom. She met a boy, and they started to date. One day she announced that she wanted to get married. That scared me. I took it hard. I think changing my attitude toward the situation and seeing it from the heart point of view will help me.

— Two of you helped each other, and, of course, it is difficult to part now. It is difficult if you don't see anything and anyone around you except her and your feelings. But there are many other things around, and if you open up to life, it will give you not one but many other people. Perhaps this will be a different kind of closeness.

— *Both of us would love to experience that. We've been through many different relationships, and we have always returned to each other.*

— You still harbor a conviction that only the two of you will be able to understand each other; no one in the entire world will ever be able to understand you.

— *Yes, this is my conviction. It's probably wrong, but …*

— It is very difficult to live this way. Why do we gather here? When we open up to each other, we get closer, and we see that other people can understand us. These people may not be our parents, husbands, or lovers, but spiritually they might be even closer to us. And there are many people like that. Every one of us can become such a human being. All of us are spiritually connected to each other; we just forgot about it. If you really know this, not just heard someone talk about it, but really understand this, life turns out to be completely different. If you know this, you as a parent will not be so strongly attached to your children. You will do everything you can for them, and you will let them go when they are ready to go. And they will go where they are supposed to go to. Those will be different relationships based on the understanding of ourselves when everyone feels, understands, and loves all other people, not just a few friends and relatives. All of us human beings are one big family.

— *Can you imagine and understand what a seventeen-year old girl hit by a car feels after spending six months in a hospital? How can you understand that if you have not experienced it yourself? I can't imagine that.*

— Every one of us goes through his own experiences. This was your experience. Everyone is given an experience that may help him understand the most important thing and to get to the level of the spiritual heart. You can get there through what happened to you. Somebody else will have a different experience, but all of us are moving in this direction. We pass through different experiences, walk different routes, experience different hardships, but we all walk in the same direction.

— *I understand that this trauma was not coincidental, but don't you think this experience was too traumatic and tragic for one's future life?*

"Why do I suffer more than anybody else?"

— I cannot agree with that. Life is immensely wise, but we can only understand its wisdom by transferring to another state of consciousness where we experience unity with everything else. We need to transition to this state of awareness. Life is very wise, and it provides us with exactly what we need to enter this unified state of consciousness. Each one of us will have his own challenges, and that's what we need. We appraise everything that happens to us based on external effects. One man is given one thing; another is given another thing. One man has a near death experience, another has his leg amputated, and the third one becomes a drug addict. You see it through the external point of view, not from the point of view from which I am discussing it. You don't understand yet that every hardship you have experienced leads you to your spiritual heart, to your essence. Yes, someone's leg was amputated, and his life became more difficult. Yes, when someone is sick, his life is harder. But what is of utmost importance in everything that happens to you? What is of utmost importance is what leads you to the center. We come here only to return to our true center. We don't come here to live a respectable, comfortable life. That would be foolish from my point of view. Then why would we need all of this? What would our evolution be about? Are we here to live a comfortable life? Why do we need this civilization? Do we only need it for people to have a nice house, a car, and a bank account? What is all of this for? It would be meaningless to live for this, I think. There is something deeper and much more beautiful here. Perhaps what each one of us experiences now is what will lead us to it. But we continue to appraise our life from the point of view of the insignificant: comfort, physical wellbeing, etc. Looking from this point of view, one is luckier while another one of us is less lucky, but this is a very superficial point of view. Deep down we are all going toward the same thing, but each one uses a different route. And each one is given exactly what he needs to get to know himself and to come to his center. Why were you given such an ordeal? You were given to experience it because it is the best experience you can have. This is what you need. Why do I have to experience this difficult situation? I must experience it because that's exactly what I need. And if you continue to resent it by saying, "Why did I have to have two legs amputated while he had only one amputated?" you will not understand anything. The ordeals we receive correspond to our strengths and teach us what we need to know.

— I want to ask you something. You asked, "Can another human being understand me if he did not experience what I experienced?" But what exactly does he need to understand, and why do you believe that another human being can understand you only by going through what you went through? Why do you think that he will not be able to understand you any other way? Do people really need to understand each other all the time? Each one of us has his own life to live. Each one of us lives it the way he lives it. We are very different. Perhaps, we should not understand each other at all. Some people go through situations that are much more difficult and painful than yours. Does it mean we need to be constantly in conflict? Does it mean we cannot understand what love and friendship is?

— I am glad you have focused our attention on this. You have asked, "How can another human being understand me?" Perhaps he will not be able to understand you, if he has not gone through what you have gone through. But is his main assignment to understand you or to understand himself? What do parents usually try to do? They try to make their child understand them. To do that, they create situations for him that they have experienced themselves, so later they can tell him, "You have gone through this yourself. Do you understand now how bad I felt? Do you understand me now?" The most important thing for every human being who comes to Earth is to understand himself through what happens to him. By limiting our child's life and creating situations for him that we cannot climb out of ourselves, we are replacing his life by our own life, which cannot be very successful, by the way. By doing that, we commit a great crime. Every human being should live his own life. Only his own life will help him

156

understand who he really is, in case he wants to understand it. When he understands who he is, he will see that we all are one. He will learn the most important thing that will allow him to understand every human being on Earth, and you in particular. A human being can understand another human being only when he understands himself. Therefore, the task of close friends and relatives is not to force another human being to understand why they feel bad, but to allow him to pursue his own life path so he can understand himself. By getting to know himself, he will understand everyone and everything.

The opposite side of a big love

— Can I tell you about my situation? My parents loved me dearly, but I was always scared of life as a child. I felt weak. I knew I would not survive on my own if I were to lose my mother. I always tried to prepare myself for some kind of a calamity. I imagined being lost in a desert without anything to eat...

I want to say that I am very happy with my mom. She is a brave woman. Notwithstanding her attachment to me, she was always mindful of my freedom and allowed me to do things on my own. Recently, I developed a desire to prove to myself that I could do something dangerous. I was able to overcome my fear. Mom, on the other hand, feels that she is to blame for my desire to run away from her. I try to explain to her that this is my inner desire. I want to learn to live. I explain that I don't blame her for anything. I am grateful to her, and I respect the courage with which she accepts life's challenges. The process of a child's separation from his/her parents is inevitable, and all of us must experience it. It does not matter what kind of a relationship we have: warm or cold. It seems to me, that if I were to have a bad relationship with my mom, I would have a less difficult time moving out to live on my own. I am dealing with the opposite extreme here. It is difficult to move away from a big love.

— Many children say that their parents did everything they could for them to move out of the house. They are upset with them and think that their parents simply wanted to throw them out. But everything here has two sides. Let's say you were overly attached to your parents, and they were also strongly attached to you. Let's say they die suddenly, and you are left on your own. Your attachments are still here, but the people they were directed toward have passed away. This shock is similar to the shock a child experiences when his umbilical cord is cut off. He lived inside Mom's body. She nourished him. Suddenly, he is thrown outside into the world. Cutting of the umbilical cord is a material reflection of this fact. The energetic connection between a mother and a child is very strong. It is transmitted through breastfeeding, physical touch, and words. It lasts for quite a long time. But the cord was cut, and a child should separate from Mom. Two bodies cannot exist as one anymore. This separation occurs in the material world, and thus, parents should prepare their children to live on their own, independently. This is the opposite side of the coin. You need to learn how to live on your own, and your parents, who were possibly rough with you since childhood, prepared you to do that, even though they might have done it without a full understanding of what they were doing. That's another side. Thanks to this behavior of your parents, you became independent earlier. You may need to work on what you have experienced a deficiency in later on, i.e. on warmth and closeness. You were thrown into life fast and had to take care of yourself right away, but you were deprived of attachment, and you will search for it. Those who have not been deprived of attachment will have to fulfill the opposite side; they will have to learn to be independent and to get to know the state of loneliness. Eventually, all of us will have to pass these stages anyway. We will have to meet every duality. We will have to balance all of them inside ourselves. Some of us encounter the left side of a given *coin* first, and then we encounter the right side later on. For others, the situation is reversed. Life is wise, and what happens to us is right and necessary for our understanding of ourselves. But when you become fixated on one side of what is happening to you without trying to understand another side, you wind up having a one-sided perception and will suffer as a result. Why blame your parents for not providing you with the second side of the *coin*? Most of the time, they cannot give you both sides. Usually people get hang up only on one side, and if they are attached to you, they are just attached to you. If they try to part with you, they do only that. To provide a child with an opportunity to understand both sides of a coin is the art of child's upbringing. A child needs to know and feel that he is loved and, at the same time, be allowed to learn how to become independent, because if he does not become independent, he will not be able to build relationships with other people as equal with equals, he will always depend on someone else. Every one of us received what he received. Most likely that was just one side. Now you need to understand the other side and to connect both sides in yourself. This is the way to your wholeness.

   — *I agree. Life is wise, and the heart is the greatest teacher. We need to turn to it more frequently. It will advise us what to do. I was born in a small Kazakh town and spent nineteen years there. It was a quiet place surrounded by steppes. I had three brothers and a sister. Mom taught us to turn to our hearts as often as we could. She used phrases such as, "Maternal heart advises me now" and "Let your heart decide" all the time. When I turned nineteen, I found myself in Moscow without any future plans. It just happened. I spent my first year living with maternal aunt. Now that it is over, I realize that this was a test. She used to tell me, "Tatiana, you live according to your heart. You cannot live like that. You don't have anything. You will not amount to much." It was very difficult to take. I am happy to say I passed this test, and I can say that my heart always advised me what to do next. I meet wonderful people, and I receive daily confirmations that I must always turn to my heart for advice.*

Can you see the Human Being in a human being?

— Some people carry thoughts and ideas that don't unite but separate people. Having these thoughts, people see others as a threat to their lives. When we start to see that we are not a compilation of these thoughts and ideas, we can look at everything that happened to us from the side. We start to understand that all these thoughts and ideas were given to us by someone, while we, not understanding what we were doing, picked them up. Those separating thoughts and ideas lead us to this awful state of internal and external disarray. Once we become aware of this, we start to see who we really are and to understand that we all are one.

— *Yes, I started to observe some changes in myself too. When I realized that I cannot hate anymore, this feeling fell off me. I was left with a warm and pleasant feeling which I had always had toward my mother.*

— I think this happens, or at least can happen, in the life of many people. A child initially perceives his parents as big, important, strong, and solid beings. Later, he suddenly sees that they are weak. He realizes they don't understand what they say. But one can go further, to see them as human beings and to start to love them. You need to understand that everything that separates us has to do with the false, illusory ideology, which we unconsciously absorbed. If we separate a human being from this ideology, we would see a Human Being. We would see a being who yearns for love but does not know how to get it. By the way, quite frequently, a child sees this better than adults and serves as the initiator of the new understanding. Perhaps the changes that a child experiences will lead to similar changes in his/her parents.

— *I think these conflicts and fights will recur a couple more times, but I see both sides now. I know them now. I previously tried to be calm about it, but I was not successful because I did not see myself. Now, I am truly calm. I started to let go off my attachments one by one. I have stepped away from many conflicts because I can see myself from the side. I see that everything is inside me.*

— The most important thing in our work is to start seeing the Human Being in a human being. We are all one. We have been fooled by the idea of our separation. We have been convinced of this illusion by certain ideologies. It is very important to separate a human being from this ideology. To see the Human Being in a human being, we need to see and understand that the ideology that separates us is based on our dependencies. When we want or don't want something badly, we get scared, and we cannot see the human being and the situation in which we are involved the way they really are. We become afraid of the possibility of a loss. As we weaken and remove our dependencies, we start to see ourselves and other people clearly. Perhaps this is what all of us are striving for.

— *I am scared to see a man who is completely open, because in that case, I have to open up myself too. This idea is inside my head. When people open up to me, I get scared because I have to open up too. I want to be open all the time, but I am afraid. These two feelings are always fighting inside me. I am still afraid to open up to my mother all the way. It is probably the most difficult thing to open up to one's parents.*

— It is difficult, but it offers you the greatest opportunity to liberate yourself. Whatever appears to be very difficult carries the greatest opportunity.

— I want to add something to the topic of openness. When two closed up human beings communicate—I am closed and he is closed—everything is normal, but when one starts to open up, the fact that another is closed becomes obvious. That's where this sharp discomfort comes from, I think, when one man starts to feel how closed he is in comparison to the one who opens up to him.

— How can you know that you are dressed? You can only know that by seeing a naked human being. The honesty of openness cannot leave you feeling indifferent. When another human being starts to open up, everything changes. You can no longer play the role you have played before. You either leave or something happens to you. Many people want their friends and relatives to be open and honest, but you cannot force anyone to do that. The only thing you can do is to do it yourself. When you start to open up to them, something will happen to them too. This is the only way to do it. If you are unhappy that your child deceives you, the reason is not in him but in you; you have taught him to do that. It is difficult to accept that, but if you are honest with yourself, another man will not be able to do what he did anymore. Therefore, a lot depends on you, on your desire to change yourself. Your changes will be accompanied by changes in the people around you. If you try to change people without changing yourself, you will not succeed. Your problems would double. If, however, you find the power inside to change yourself, this power will change the people next to you too. There is no other way to do it.

CHAPTER 5
WANT AND CAN

You have been told also that life is darkness, and in your weariness
you echo what was said by the weary.
And I say that life is indeed darkness save when there is urge,
And all urge is blind save when there is knowledge,
And all knowledge is vain save when there is work,
And all work is empty save when there is love;
And when you work with love you bind yourself to yourself, and to
one another, and to God.

—Kahlil Gibran, *The Prophet, On Work*

Do you really want that?

— How can we come to understand what we want?

— *I want to learn how to sing. I don't want to be afraid to say nasty
things to people. I want to be sure of myself. I want to learn to love.*

— *I am hungry all the time, but I am also lazy, and I don't want to
cook. I want to receive pleasure every minute of my life. I don't want to be
afraid of anything. I want my life to be exciting and challenging.*

— *I want to read Castaneda's books. I want to look impressive.*

— *I want to aquire inner calmness. I want to have a job that would
allow me to do what I think is necessary to do, i.e. to realize my ideas and
to be paid well for it.*

— I want to go mountain climbing. I've wanted to do that for a very long time, but something always interferes. I want to go to a theater, but somehow, I am unable to do that either. I want to have self-control.

— I am quite modest in my desires now, but I still have quite a few of them. I used to live with a slogan: "To fight, to search, to find and enjoy." But now I find that the most important thing is not to grab, but to retain.

— Have you notice that everyone told us what he or she wants? How does a human being speak of his desire if it is strong? The way you speak of your desire can tell us a lot about the power of this desire. Many people say that they want this and they want that. Sometimes I listen to people, and I think, "Do you really want that?" And who really wants it? Is it you who really wants it? Is it really your desire, or did you just hear it somewhere? If everybody wants a red Mustang convertible, I want it too. It is not easy to determine what your real desires are. And what moves you? Where do you take energy from and how do you express it? It is precisely the power, depth, and spectrum of one's desire that determines the way that human being lives, whether he does something or not, whether he can do anything or not. The life of a human being, who is limited by the desire to have a dog, will differ from the life of someone who desperately wants to invent something. So, which of the desires you stated is really yours? Look at the list of your desires from this point of view.

Why do you want what you want?

— What you really want is always with you. So, what is it that you really want?

— I want to have my own appartment, and I want to learn to love.

— What would your own apartment give you?

— *It will allow me to live away from my parents.*

— And what will the opportunity to live away from your parents offer you?

— *It will offer me an opportunity to live with someone I want to live with.*

— And what will the opportunity to live with someone you want to live with offer you?

— *...?*

— I ask you these questions to help you sort out your main desire and to see what's behind it. Quite frequently a human being talks about something believing it to be his desire when something else is behind it. Why do I need a new apartment? It is not an apartment that most people need, but the opportunity to be by themselves. Perhaps they need this opportunity to be by themselves to become aware of something. Quite frequently people get mixed up in their desires. They say, "I want this." But why do they need it? People seldom ask this question. A man wants a car. Why does he need it? Someone wants a car to show how successful he is. Another man wants a car to drive somewhere and to free his mind from what is happening in his life now. For the third one, a car is an opportunity to travel. Meanwhile, all three of them talk about a car, even though their desires are different.

How well do you know what you really want? What stands behind what you call your desire? What is your strongest desire?

— *I want to have a will power. I have been very unorganized since childhood, and I want to become self-collected.*

— And why do you want to become self-collected?

— *In order to do everything I want.*

— And what exactly do you want to do?

— *I want to take care of my health. I have to do that, but I am lazy.*

165

— You want to have the will power to start to take care of your health? And why do you need to be healthy?

— *What do you mean, why do I need to be healthy? I think everyone wants to be healthy.*

— Is health your aim?

— *No, it is not my aim. It is the means.*

— And what exactly is it a means for?

— *It is a means for life.*

— So, you want to live?

— *But, of course.*

— So you need to be healthy in order to live.

— *Yes, I need to be healthy in order to live.*

— And what does it mean to live? How do you want to live? Do you live now?

— *I live now, but when one is sick, one's life is sort of ... I don't want to spend my life in a hospital. I want to have strength to enjoy life in all its manifestations.*

— So, you dont want to be sick. **Observe how frequently people talk not about what they want, but about what they don't want.** "I don't want to be sick." But what does it mean to be healthy? People have totally different things in mind when they talk about health. One says, "I want to be healthy because I want to compete in the Olympics. Another says, "I am healthy when I can do the work I love to do, when my body helps me to do my work."

How to formulate your desire?

— Do you think it is important to be able to formulate your desire? We frequently use such words and notions as, "I want to be free." What does it mean to be free? It is one thing when this is said by someone who is in jail for life, and a totally different thing when it is said by someone who just got married, or who has been married for fifteen years, or by a child who wants to go to the movies but is forbidden to do so. Each one of them have used the same word *freedom*, but each one of them has a totally different notion of what it means. We frequently say words without trying to figure out what they mean exactly. But where can we go and what can we get if we don't know exactly what we want? For example, what is will power? Some people say, "I don't have the willpower to learn anything." I ask them, "What exactly do you want to learn?" — "I don't know exactly, but I want to learn in general." A man does not know what he wants to learn, and he is surprised that he is unable to learn it. **Unless you formulate your aim properly, you will not get the energy necessary to achieve it. If you don't see what you want clearly, you will not be able to get it. You start to approach your aim when you start to understand your true desire.** Perhaps what you call the absence of free will is not exactly what you think it is. Perhaps this is the imprecision in your understanding of your own desires.

— *I don't think so. In my case, I know exactly what I need to do, but I don't have enough power to do it.*

— Is it possible that you **really** don't want to do it very much? Who can recall a situation when he clearly knew what he wanted, wanted it badly, but was not successful in accomplishing it?

— *If we take this approach, it follows that I don't want anything.*

— Yes, that's exactly what follows. It appears to me that willpower, the way you see it, is necessary for you to overcome something you don't want to do. For example, it is necessary for me to exercise in the morning. I understand that I need to exercise, but I don't want to do that. In that case, I have to use my willpower to force myself to do it. But what if I want to do it? What if exercise brings me pleasure? What if I wake up in the morning full of desire to go for a run? Do I need willpower in that case? Do I need willpower when this activity brings me pleasure and my body wants to experience it? My body leads me to put a pair of running shoes on and to go for a run. I want, and I know what I want. In that case, I don't need any additional willpower.

— *Using this logic, we can come to the conclusion that I don't want to live, but this is not the case.*

— How do you know that this is not the case? Many people don't want to live. They live just out of habit. They live just because they were born, and, therefore, need to live. We are being told daily that we need to survive. We need to survive. If you take this statement apart, you will see that the notion behind it is that life is difficult and dangerous, and therefore, you need to survive. We don't need to live and to be happy. No, we need to survive. The accent is placed not on something pleasant and interesting that we want to do, but on something unpleasant and not interesting that needs to be done. The absence of honest and true desires leads many people to think of the willpower they need in order to do something that they don't want to do but what needs to be done. Quite frequently, man's desires do not come out of his essence but are forced on him. He would not have done it if he was not forced to do it. Naturally, in this case, he does not have a strong energy or desire to do it. But, as he does not know what he really wants, he continues to do what he does without pleasure. Please, write down your true desires here right now:

_____

_____

_____

_____

_____

_____

Do you want to have your own apartment, or do you want to have solitude?

— *I have been bothered by a very strong desire for a long time. I want to have my own apartment. I want to feel that it is mine. I want to know that no one can throw me out of it. I want to have some kind of stability. It seems to me that this is a very strong desire, but presently, I cannot fulfil it. I can't do anything about it.*

— So, you want to have an apartment. How will your state change when you get an apartment?

— *I will know that it is mine. I will feel calm.*

— What prevents you from feeling calm now? What prevents you from feeling calm in the condition you happen to be in now?

— *When I start to think about the future, I realize that the time will come when I will not be able to share a room with other people. What will I do? Where will I go with my child? I feel scared.*

— You explain your living in fear now by not having your own apartment. Let's imagine you have your own apartment. Would that alleviate your fear? Would you not worry about losing it? I know many people who have lost their apartments and houses. The presence of an apartment does not guaranty calmness. So, what can you do now to be calm? Is it possible for you to be calm without living in your own apartment?

— *I can stop thinking about the future. I can live in the present moment. Sometimes, I can do that.*

— What if we were to give an apartment to a restless, stressed, and scared human being? Will he immediately become calm, happy, and self-assured?

— *No, I dont think so. I am very familiar with the fear of being homeless. This fear does not disappear when one buys his own apartment. This is my experience. By the way, I just saw my desire. I want to become aware of the border: mine vs. others. I am in constant imbalance. I either open up to a point that every passerby can spit into my Soul, or I build such a wall around myself that no one can penetrate.*

— Yes, I have heard you speak about it many times. You spoke about your desire to have your own place. You even spoke of a car as a place in which you can take refuge to be by yourself. By the way, many people see their cars as a place they can be amongst people and at the same time to be separated from them. You are driving in traffic; you are at the same time with others and in your own enclosed space. This desire appears in connection to your desire to be with people and your fear of being hurt by them. You had experienced these situations, and this memory remains engraved in you. On one side, you are facing a desire to open up and share your life with someone. On the other side, you desire to put up a barrier and separate yourself from every possible insult. At the same time, we say that this is a desire to buy an apartment or a car. This desire requires a lot of energy. At the present time, an apartment is one of the most expensive purchases a man can make, and if a man does not clearly understand what he really wants, he invests all his energy into buying an apartment. He works a lot. The work by itself creates many difficulties, but his main problem does not get solved. Moreover, it exacerbates.

— *I share a room with two other people. Seven adults are living together in this three-bedroom apartment, and I frequently get mad at my roommates. When that happens, I really want to be on my own, in my own apartment. But sometimes, during very bad moments, I am grateful to God that I am not on my own. I know many people who have their own cars, apartments, and houses and suffer because of it. They envy my bohemian lifestyle and my ability to move from one place to another at any moment.*

Don't confuse the means with an aim

— We frequently confuse the means with the aim. And, by the way, the means that we have are usually given to us by the outside world. Look at what happens to a human being when he receives what he thinks he needs to have. Your recent answers demonstrated a certain standard set of desires: "I want to have my own apartment, I want to have a well-paying job, I want to have the money." Look around you. There are people who have it all. By the way, many of them don't desire anything anymore. So, what does a man really want? Does he really want what he says he wants? Does he really understand what is behind this "I want"? Some people say, "I want", pursue what they want, and get it. Others say, "I want", and don't follow up on it. What do they get later on? Do they get what's important for them, or do they continue to do something that doesn't bring them closer to their aim for many years, only later realizing that they did not really need it?

Aspiration is very important. I would like to review this in detail. Man's desires frequently do not correspond to his real needs. However, he does something and applies effort to get it. It is precisely this activity that gives him strength. Who usually gets sick the most? It is people who are idle, who don't do anything, and the retired people who get sick the most. Many retired people continue to work today. We did not see it before. Men used to deteriorate very fast after retirement. A man was doing some kind of work all his life. He loved his work. Then he would retire and age very fast. In two or three years, he would turn into an old man. Why does this happen? It happens because he does not have the old energy anymore. He is not occupied with the work that used to bring him pleasure. He starts to get sick. Many of these retirees would find "work" in their diseases. They would go to doctors. They would spend weeks in hospitals. Disease turned out to be very important for them. When a human being does not have anything in his life, he stops living. He needs to find something to do. If he does not have anything positive in life, he finds something negative. In that case, he starts to act out of principle: "I don't want that." For example, I don't want people to bother me, and I start to fight everyone around me. Another one says, "I don't want these people to come to power," joins the opposite party and starts to fight them. Why? What for? What does it give him? Many people live like this without understanding what they do and what they want. Some people don't do anything at all. They deteriorate. They sink into drugs and alcohol. Those are their ways to get away from themselves. If you don't see anything here, you try to go to another world. But you are unlikely to find anything there if you cannot find anything here. So, your strongest desires are:

_____

_____

_____

_____

_____

_____

— *I experience brief episodes of wanting something badly. During these moments, I feel an energy surge. I feel strong. But there are also periods when I don't want anything. I feel completely drained of energy. During such moments, I can think of suicide. What am I to do then?*

— It's unnatural for a human being not to have a desire to live, because there is nothing but life here. There is nothing greater than life. When a man denies life, he denies everything. It is very difficult to live in such a state. But behind this lack of desire to live, from my point of view, is simply not understanding of what you are living for. You may be experiencing such a period in your life now. Many people experience it at some point in their lives. This period offers you an opportunity to contemplate what you are living for. A new man can be born out of this state—a man who knows what he wants. A man has an opportunity to be reborn. This opportunity to be reborn to life is given to us because it is unnatural to deny life.

"Let me have my peace, but don't let me be alone"

— *I can describe how I've been feeling lately in one sentence: "Let me have my peace, but don't let me be alone." At the same time, I have a strong desire to belong to myself irrespective of everything. I belong to society, to the people I communicate with, to my parents, but I don't belong to myself. I do not feel that I belong to myself.*

— A human being harbors two tendencies. One tendency is to be by himself; this frequently leads to a desire to separate from people and to go deep inside oneself. Another tendency manifests itself as a desire to be amongst people. These two tendencies frequently come head to head and one goes crazy: "What do I do now? Do I stay by myself or do I stay with people? But if I am with people, where am I? They ask me to do things, and they are with me only because I comply with their desires. If I don't do what they want, I will be on my own. This is scary."

— *How can one be amongst people and not dissolve in them? How can one remain whole? How can I be myself?*

— A man should spend some time on his own. If a group of people constantly surrounds you, you will never be able to part with the illusions of this particular group of people. For example, you came to a company where people drink a lot. They have their values, and you can get lost amongst these illusory values. They tell you, "Have a drink. Have another drink." They think drinking brings them closer. What brings people closer? People constantly try to get close to each other, but because many of them don't understand who they are and what is important to them, they use habitual for them methods to get closer. In reality, these methods have nothing to do with deep, truly human communication. Some people unite around a bottle of alcohol. You have probably seen these people. What makes them come together? A human being cannot be alone for a long time. He gets scared. He tries to get together with other people. He needs to find something in common with these people. Some people gather around a bottle of alcohol, while others get together based on some political agenda. They start to fight other people, but they end up fighting themselves. Does what people unite around really what connects them, or do they unite around something illusory and fictitious? Does a union which is based on such norms and values bring a sensation of real closeness or, on the contrary, lead to separation? What brings people together? Do they gather to understand themselves, to open up and see that we all are one? We are one because what connects us all is inside us. The words themselves, associating with different notions in those who pronounce them and those who hear them, frequently separate people from each other, from their common essence. There is no shortage of so-called religious and psychological organizations nowadays, but how many people in these organizations really feel close to each other? United in an organization, they feel close to its members, but they feud with people who don't belong to this organization. What is it that unites them? Is it something real or another illusory notion that will eventually separate them again?

— *What about family as a unifying structure? Sometimes, it turns into a closed system that has no connections with the outside world. It is almost impossible for a human being to remain himself within it. A certain hierarchy is created in every family with a system of values that quite frequently is totally separated from the rest of the world. What can we do about a family?*

What can we do about a family?

— It is not correct to say that a system of values is created in a family that is different from society. What do people in a family unit usually want? What do people usually talk about when they get together to create a family? They usually talk about having a nice house and making a good living. They speak about kids and how to get kids through college and make sure they have a decent living. When we speak of families, we usually speak of families with children. If a man and a woman, who don't have children, suddenly feel that they don't want to live together any longer, they separate easier than people who have kids. Quite frequently kids obligate parents to continue their cohabitation, even when they don't what to live together anymore. What kind of norms and reasons force them to pull this heavy burden of married life then?

— *Family reflects the norms and values of a society.*

— Perhaps I did not make myself clear. That was not what I wanted to emphasize. I meant to say that family is a closed system in which one can easily dissolve. And, as it happens to be a concentrated unit of society, it is even more difficult to live in it than to live within society.

— It is not without a reason that people say that the family is a unit of a society. When society wants to get stronger, it first starts to reinforce the family institution. When society starts to break up, families start to break up too. You can observe these tendencies in many countries around the globe.

Do we even need a family? Do we need a family the way it currently exists? What do people unite into the families for? We can investigate this topic from different points of view. What exactly concerns you?

— I am interested in that special period of time when husband and wife give birth to children, and when their feelings toward each other start to change. I am talking about my own family, of course. My parents are not connected to each other by anything outside of habit nowadays. They still live together. They don't know how to live differently. I live with them, and their relationship affects me. I am being fed, clothed, and taken care of, but in return, I am being constantly asked to confirm that I am their property.

— Exactly. We started our conversation by discussing desires. Let's look at the family unit from this point of view. What are the desires that unite people to form a family? Which of these desires gets realized and which don't? When the desires of two human beings who united and formed a family do not get realized, it naturally starts to affect their child. That's why many people don't want to get married nowadays. Until now, neither one of you have expressed a desire to have a child, and this confirms what I just said. Perhaps you don't want to have a child because of the difficulties associated with bringing another human being into this world.

So what kind of desires unite people into families? Why aren't these desires realized? It is precisely the fact that these desires don't get realized that leads to conflict and a high level of stress in families. Both the bride and the groom were looking for someone to join and share their "not" understanding of life with. You can say that I exaggerate, but that's what it is, in reality. People frequently unite precisely for this reason. For example, a young woman doesn't want to stay with her parents because they suffocate her. She wants freedom, but she doesn't have the money to be on her own. In such situations, young people frequently search for someone who will provide for them. Some run away from home. The main desire that leads them is the desire to avoid a negative experience: "I feel bad here. I have to run away from here." One of the best ways to run away is to get married. Many people don't get married, they run into marriage. As a result, everything goes awry, because their desire was to run away. And they both run away. Two human beings who run from something get together. What united them was their desire to run away. Eventually, they would want to run away from each other too, but first they will have to abuse each other with their mutual "not" understanding of what they did and why they did it. Eventually, everything becomes visible. They start to suffer and torture each other. They may not understand why this is happening to them. They feel bad here, and they try to run to a place where, as it appears to them, they will feel better. But the situation is going to repeat itself, because their real desire is to run away from what is bad, not to find what is good. You can only find goodness when you understand what is going on. But you need to understand it. When you feel bad, you just try to run away. It is difficult to understand what you really want. In order to do that, you need to see what you do all the time. Why do you do that? What do you want to achieve by doing that? What do you get? Most people don't want to understand. Thus, they constantly run away from what they don't want, never getting to where they really want to be, because they don't know what they really want. What you are discussing now is not a dead-end situation. There are no dead-end situations here. It happens to be a dead-end until you come to understand what is happening to you and what you really want. If you come to understand what you really want now, you will be able to do it. So, what do you really want?

Why don't you try to answer this question right here and right now:

_____

_____

_____

_____

_____

_____

_____

— *I want to solve the inner conflict that has been bothering me for a long time.*

— In order to solve this, you need to understand what you **really** want. If you just want to resolve a conflict, you will continue to occupy yourself with it all the time. Your parents will offer you multiple opportunities to do that. You will spend many years trying to sort out what is happening to them. If, on the other hand, you become aware of what you really want, the situation will change instantly. Your parents did what they did. They did it themselves. You can try to leave, but where will you go? What kind of thoughts and desires will you harbor? Those are important questions. It is not hard to leave, but...

— *That's why I dont leave. I know that my leaving them will not solve the problem.*

— But if you stay, you need to understand why you are staying.

— *That's why I want to sort it out.*

— So, let's sort it out. What do you **really** want?

— *I want to understand why it's in me and how to get it out.*

— What is "it"? What is "it" that does not satisfy you in your family? You said you cannot be by yourself.

— *I have been offered an opportunity to be by myself.*

— Do you know who you really are?

— *No, they don't allow me to understand myself.*

— And how can you be yourself, if you don't know who you really are? Does it make any difference whether your parents provide you with this opportunity or not? How can you be what you want to be if you don't know who you are? And if you know who you are, who can prevent you from being it?

— *Okay. In that case, I want to understand who I am.*

— Great. But in that case, how is this connected to your family? You just said that it is precisely your family that prevents you from understanding of who you are. Look at how easy it is to get distracted from a question you need to solve. This is the most difficult question: to understand who I really am. You can try to understand it yourself, or you can blame others for preventing you from understanding it. In this case, you spend all your energy on blame, trying to explain why you are not allowed to be who you are.

— *I did not say that. I don't blame anyone.*

— Yes, but you started with your family.

— I did not start with my family. I finished with it. I spoke for a long time, and I finished with a family, because this is the last part of the equation.

— Perhaps it is precisely the family that will help you understand who you really are. Your family members force you to think about this question. Few people think about this unless some external forces awaken them to it. Most people start to do something only when they are forced to. **A man can become aware of what's going on with him only when he acts and does something tangible in the material world, irrespective of whether he was forced to do it or not.** In that case, everything that happens to him, works for him.

There are no good circumstances or bad circumstances; everything here is an opportunity. Every situation you happen to be in is the best opportunity for you to become aware of what you really need. First, you need to understand that a situation in which you found yourself is an opportunity for you to understand something. Second, you must know what exactly you want to understand. In this case, you will be able to use any situation in which you happen to find yourself. You can use any situation, even the most horrible situation, to become aware of yourself. Moreover, the more dramatic the situation is, the better opportunity it offers you to understand something about yourself. You must have a strong intention to understand it.

— I think I want that already. I keep thinking and talking about it.

— Then you need to start walking in that direction.

— I do. I took my first step when I decided not to leave. My first impulse was to leave, but I did not. I stayed in order to understand myself.

How can you see, hear, and feel your desire?

— We spoke of human desires. If a man does not want anything, he is dead. He does not have any energy. He is not there. When a man starts to become aware of himself, he returns to life and action. Desires start to awaken in him. These can be desires that were forced on him or desires that are truly his own. Most people do something not because they want to do it, but because they are bound by certain norms, or someone has told them what to do. This is better than doing nothing but worse than doing something you really want to do yourself. For some people, to do something is an opportunity to start to understand what they really want. You start to do something, and suddenly you see that what you do does not really attract you. In that case, you try to figure out and understand what is it that you really want to do. When you finally start to sense, see, and feel what you truly desire, even if this desire is distant and foggy, at least this desire comes from you.

A question arises now: "How am I to do what I really want to do?" If you really have a desire that comes from your deepest essence, how are you to see it, to feel and hear it? How can you clarify this desire of yours? "I just want to go somewhere," a man says. It's irrelevant for him where he goes: west, east, north, or south; to the woods or to the nearest town. But at least he wants to go somewhere. He is ready to act, but where is he going? It is not clear to him or the people around him. "Where are you going?" you ask him. "Well, I want to get somewhere," he says. You ask him, "Where exactly do you want to get to? Let's try to see it. Perhaps, we can hear it. Perhaps, we can feel it." Let's try to sort out and formulate clearly what exactly you really want. Perhaps your desire has not been formed yet. Perhaps it is foggy. Let's make it clear. Let's do it right now:

_____

_____

_____

_____

_____

_____

_____

— *What if my desire is determined not by where I am to go, but by whom I am to go with?*

— You have to be more precise. You must formulate your desire better.

— *I have a friend who is a speleologist. His desire is to hitchhike to different places and to explore caves. I have never experienced a desire to descend deep down into the Earth, but he was so enthusiastic about it that I thought to myself, "I am going for it. Next time I am going with you." But it just dawned on me, do I really want to get down there, or do I just want to be next to him?"*

— Did this desire come out of him? Did he verbalize it to you?

— *Yes, he was very animated. He was talking about it and showing me pictures. This desire came to me from the outside. It was not forced on me. It was a gift from him. Hmm… He descends into the caves now, but where is he going to go next? Will I also want to go with him then?*

— He can walk into a burning house or jump from a skyscraper. Is it love if you were to join him?

— *I have said earlier that I want an apartment, and I want my husband to quit drinking, but it turns out, I don't accept him the way he is and he does not accept me the way I am. He has built an image of a woman he loves, but this is not me.*

— "The sober one will never understand the one who is drunk."

— *Exactly, a man who whose belly is full cannot understand a starving man. My desire is to accept people the way they are. In other words, I will not need to have my own apartment, because I will constantly remember how bad I felt when I was alone. I don't want to be alone. In reality, my desire is not for people to be the way I want them to be, but for me to accept them the way they are, and for people to accept me the way I am.*

— Amazing. Suddenly, everything has changed. Here is a man who happens to be a husband and who drinks every other day. And there is nothing, apparently, more horrible than this if our goal is to be calm and not to be bothered by it. But when we start to understand what we really want, it turns out that we want to accept people the way they are. This may be one of our most important assignments, because if we learn to do that, life will become totally different. If we learn to do that, everything around us will make us happy. We will find something amazing and beautiful in everything. What pleasant things can I find in this man, if I don't accept him when he is drunk? If that is the case, every time he is close to me, I am in a horrible state. And as he is constantly around me, I am constantly in a horrible state. Therefore, I must do something in order not to see him. But eventually, another similar man will come to replace him. Therefore, I am left with an amazing aim—to learn to accept life, events, and people the way they are, and to see myself in them, because what we reject in other people is what we really reject in ourselves. You will start to see that if you want to. **What irritates us in other people more than anything is what irritates us more than** anything in ourselves. **But we don't want to see our character flaws. We project them onto other people and hate in them what we hate in ourselves.** If you take a good look around, you will see that this is exactly what is happening. It is very difficult to see something in yourself, but when you start to see it in other people, you will be able to see it in yourself. For example, an aggressive man does not like and has a difficult time tolerating the aggression of other people. But he never accepts his own aggression. He says, "You are aggressive. You irritate me when you scream." Another man, for example, is very sad. He likes to cry. But when someone next to him starts to cry, he starts to feel bad. He says, "Don't cry. Please, do anything you want, but don't cry." This does not bother other people. Why? This happens because whatever we don't like in other people is what we don't like and don't accept in ourselves. **Therefore, to accept a flaw in another human being is to accept something in yourself. And if we formulate our desire in the form of this assignment, everything will turn out to be interesting and helpful.** You will start to see deep meaning in everything that happens. The human being next to you will suddenly turn into a beautiful opportunity to understand yourself. The human being who used to irritate you will suddenly turn into your best teacher. That's exactly what will happen.

Moreover, when we start to accept and understand ourselves, the people next to us start to feel that something unusual is happening to us. When we really start to change, everything around us starts to change too. You cannot force your surroundings to change, but by changing yourself you change everything around you. This is not a fast process, but it is beautiful.

Escape from oneself

— *Freedom walks hand in hand with solitude. I would even go further to say that freedom is solitude. I saw a cartoon in which a man was trying to solve a serious science problem. He wanted to be by himself. He would go deep under water, but divers and submarines would get in his way. He would go to the desert, but camels and Bedouins would interrupt his solitude. He would go to the deserted beach, but people would come there too. He could not concentrate anywhere. Finally, he got onto a spaceship, went to another planet, and solved his puzzle there. Eureka! He imagined people carrying him on their hands and singing songs about him. He ran one way—no one was there. He ran another way—no one was there either. He could not share his discovery with anyone.*

Actually, I have always had a strong desire to travel, to see something new. Professionally, I don't do what I want to do; I do what I am forced to do. I am a gold miner. I travel all over the country on business. I see beautiful places. Hmm … It just dawned on me, I have realized my desire to travel in this way.

— Great. I want to say a couple of words about this desire to travel. Many people have this desire nowadays and can fulfill it. Tourism is a fast-growing industry in our country and abroad. I wonder about what travelers search for? What makes them travel? Perhaps they just try to find something new in the external world? They don't look inside; they look outside. I went through a period when I travelled a lot. I don't have this need to travel anymore. I am not against it. I am quite happy to get up and go, but I don't have a need to travel anymore because I saw what's inside me. What I have there is much more interesting. I have everything there. I can travel inside into my own essence now. I don't need to go anywhere to do that. I don't need to spend thousands of dollars on plane tickets and accommodations. I can travel anytime I want, and I can see, hear, and learn things the best travel agencies can't offer. Their assortment of services is quite limited: to ascend a pyramid in Egypt, to explore holy places, to get a suntan on a nice beach. That's what attracts people. I don't say no to that. I am just trying to show you that traveling is just another way to escape yourself. When you start to travel inside yourself, you find worlds and opportunities there that no one else can offer you.

— *Traveling provides me with an opportunity to prove to myself that I can overcome the calamities of nature.*

— And what for? Why do you need to prove to yourself that you can, for example, sleep on nails?

— *I don't need to prove it. I just want to find out what I am capable of. You spoke of desires. One should not desire what one cannot get. A man should check himself and find out what he can and cannot do and then decide to desire it or not to desire it. It's better not to desire something that you can't get.*

— Some men and women constantly try to prove their title of being a "man" or a "woman."

— *And why should not we check ourselves out all the time? Why do all mountain climbers try to conquer the highest cliffs? Do they run away from themselves?*

— I think many of them do. Why does one climb Everest? People cheer for him, but some housewife, cooking in her kitchen, does not understand it. She says, "What was that for? There are so many beautiful things around. Here is a child. He is laughing. He could not talk yesterday, and today he said his first word." She finds it strange that people climb mountains while other people cheer the man who conquered Everest.

— *But the man who climbed it understands why he did that.*

— I am not sure about that. Perhaps he tried to run away from himself. I don't like to talk about abstract people, but if we started this conversation, I will tell you in a certain abstract way that I have an inkling that this is the way for some people to run away from themselves.

— *I live in a city. I love nature and the countryside, but I don't have a country house.*

— And what will a country house offer to you that the city cannot?

— *I breathe easier there. The air is cleaner there.*

— What happens to you when you breathe easier? Why do you feel better because of it? Some people like cities with their exhaust pipes. They have a difficult time being in other places. They feel dizzy walking in the woods.

— *You contradict yourself. We are born to live, and we must live a full life.*

— What do you mean "we must"? Who must?

— *The one who must live must be healthy.*

— And who must live?

— *Everyone must live!*

— What does it mean to be healthy? Why do you say that it is necessary to be healthy? Why do only a few people take care of themselves and are healthy if health is so beautiful by itself? Why do so many people only start to look after themselves when they are told that they need to be healthy? Where does this desire to be healthy come from? Does it come from, "I must" or from "I want to"?

— *I want to. I want to breath fresh air. I want to swim in clean water.*

— So, do it.

— *I just realized that many of my problems are due to the fact that I don't accept myself. You are right. I must accept myself to begin with. But how do I do that?*

Acceptance through action

— You will find it is not easy to accept yourself. How can you do that if you don't know who you are? That's why I say that in order to understand who you are, you need to act. There are different ways to understand who you are. We spoke about some of them. According to the eastern approach, a man can reach his essence through deep meditation. But few eastern people can reach such depth. Many people try to, but few actually come to understand themselves that way. You get into a lotus position, you close your eyes, and you start to meditate. That does not guarantee that you will meet yourself. You can just replay the scenes and scenarios fixed in your mind. That's what usually happens. This is not a real meditation. It's a variation of sleep. Meditation is a great way to understand yourself, but most westerners don't understand what it is. What they try to do usually leads to another misunderstanding. They see some images and play with the illusions. This is a fantasy. They don't come to understand themselves better. That's why I think that the most productive way for the western man to get to know himself is through action. One can do something without awareness and with awareness. When you do something without awareness, you probably do not do what you really want to do, not what comes from the inside but what is being forced on you by the external milieu. You are told, "You have to work! You have to make money! You have to do work that will be paid for!" You finally start to earn money. Now, you need a house, and this house should be comparable to other people's houses. You also need a car. Later, it turns out you need a country house. These desires did not come from you. They were forced on you. But when you start to do something within a state of awareness, you start to understand whether you really need it or not. Perhaps you need something totally different, something that most people are not going to understand or appreciate. When you start to paint, they say, "What are you doing? You will never be a painter. You will never make a living out of it." You reply, "So, what? I want to paint because I like it." Someone else starts to sculpt. Another one just digs in the soil and plants something, not because this will bring him money, but because he expresses himself this way. In doing that, he starts to understand who he really is and what he really wants. But to do what you really want to do, you need to step away from what was forced upon you. You must refuse it, even if only partially at first. You need to allocate some time to what your heart really wants. But most people are so fixated on doing what was imposed on them that they say, "Well, I actually wanted to do something before, but I don't want to do it now. I don't know. I do what I do because a man has to do something. I need to make money right now. I will decide later." Such a man hurry-scurry and runs around but does not do much. He is constantly short of money. When he finally saves some money, he buys a car or a country home. You ask him, "Do you need all of this?" — "Stop it," he says, "What are you talking about? I am doing something right now, and I have many other things to do. I have so many things on my mind." One problem leads to another. This is an eternal circle. Meanwhile, he never gets to do what he really wanted to do. Perhaps he felt something when he was a kid, but he has forgotten about it. Return to your childhood. Recall what you felt then. Recall what you felt and start to do it. Perhaps in doing that you will understand who you are and why you are here.

— As a child, I would start on many different projects, but I would soon quit. Mom used to scream at me, "You don't finish anything!" That led to fear. I am afraid to try anything new now. I think about whether I will finish it or not, whether I should try it or not. Is there a connection between a man dropping what he started to do and the fact that he is not occupied with what is really his?

— This may be the case or not. When a man does something that he understands, he does it with full awareness. But few people can say that they really understand what they do.

You can use household chores that you do not want to do to develop your ability to control your attention and apply your effort correctly. It is very important to know how to apply your effort correctly. A man who doesn't know how to apply his effort correctly will never succeed at anything. Some people try to walk the spiritual path, refusing the physical world where they didn't learn to do anything. They say, "I will achieve here, in the spiritual realm!" I doubt that, because if a man cannot apply his efforts correctly in the physical world, he will not be able to move in a spiritual direction either, as it is more difficult than any business. If a man cannot do something simple, how can he do something that is much more difficult? If a man cannot run a hundred yards, how can he run a marathon? If a man cannot carry a four-gallon bottle of water from his house to his neighbor's house, how can we expect him to become a mountain climber? But many people flatter themselves and entertain this illusion.

The ability to apply your effort correctly and to do something with awareness, i.e. with the exact understanding of what you are doing, is very important. **Any work can be used as an opportunity to become aware and to understand yourself. I repeat, any work can be used as an**

opportunity to become aware and to understand yourself.
Any work that you do with awareness will take you to yourself.
Why do some people start something and then quit? That
happens because they do it mechanically. If you start to do the
same thing in full awareness of what you do, you will receive a
lot. You will see yourself. The work carried in full awareness
will return you to yourself. Let's take the simple work of
digging a ditch. Dig a ditch somewhere. Do it with awareness,
and you will get closer and closer to yourself with your every
move. The same can be said about washing the dishes or
cleaning the floor. People frequently try to avoid these chores
and dump them onto others. Family quarrels frequently start
because these tasks are seen as unpleasant and humiliating
rather than interesting. But done with awareness, they can
teach you a lot.

Washing dishes—a meditation for the entire family

— In any work that you do, you can find the reason for
doing it, i.e. you can find the essence of the work you do. If
you were to scrub the floors just because no one else wants to
scrub them, you would do it with anger and dissatisfaction. If,
on the other hand, you were to do it for your environment to
be cleaner or to make someone happy, this work would have a
totally different meaning. What kind of meaning do we assign
to our work? This is very important. Everything depends on
the meaning we assign to our work. If I do something I
consider uninteresting, boring, and humiliating, I would not
want to continue. If I understand why I do it, everything
changes. Look around. Quite a few people scrub floors
nowadays. Some of them have college degrees but cannot find

work in their fields. They need to earn money somehow, and that's why they do this work. Do you think many of them scrub the floors smiling happily, or do they see every passerby as a hindrance, as someone who can throw more garbage on the floor and make their job more difficult? Most of them see people as a hindrance. As a result, their faces are frequently distorted with anger. They are cleaning the floors. What can be more beautiful than making your environment clean? So, why do they do it with such angry faces? And how many other, so-called "not-prestigious" jobs are out there? Any type of work can make a man happy if he understands why he is doing it and for whom he is doing it. A man who scrubs the floor and is full of irritation does not understand who he is doing it for and often thinks about being underpaid. Thus, he is constantly unhappy. He does not understand that he is doing it for the people who walk around him, who will be happier and better off because of the work that he does.

— *It seems to me, from the effort we have to apply to accomplish something, we have returned to the question of will power. This is a vicious circle: to have will power, one has to have a strong desire. In this case, one's inner reserves open up. But to have a desire, one has to have will power.*

— If you have a strong desire to do something, the question of will power does not arise. If you don't have a strong desire to do something, this question arises. In that case, you have to force yourself to do something that you don't want to do. If you know how to activate and organize yourself, you manifest will power. Even when you do the work that you love, you sometimes go through periods of tiredness and fatigue. You like what you do, but you still can wake up tired. However, the work still needs to be finished. In that case, you must manifest a certain inner effort to complete what you have started. So, you need to know how to activate and organize yourself. This is like a second wind. A man is running. He feels he is going to fall from exhaustion at any moment. But if he perseveres and continues to run, soon he will get a second wind. But for it to come, he needs to experience a very difficult period. It is useless to develop will power for itself. You go to the gym and exercise every day. You build up powerful muscles, but when someone asks you, "What are going to do now?" you answer, "I don't know. I think I am going to work on embroidery." "Why did you build such powerful muscles then?" — "I don't know. All my friends did it. I was just following them."

You need to understand the meaning behind what you do. Some people occupy themselves with perfection for perfection's sake. They say, "I can do things that no one can do. I can stand on my left leg for two hours." They train their will power for will power's sake. But what's the meaning of it? Why do I talk so much about the true aim and true desire that comes from the essence of a human being? I do so because it is precisely this desire that brings meaning to everything we do. If we understand and are aware of it, everything we need will come to us. If a man's aim is big, he needs to have the strength and the skills to reach it. And they will come to him in due time. But if he does not have this aim, what is he living for?

CHAPTER 6
DIFFICULT PERIODS AND CHANGES
IN YOUR LIFE

•◆•

Your pain is the breaking of the shell that encloses your understanding. Even as the stone of the fruit must break, that its heart may stand in the sun, so must you know pain.

And could you keep your heart in wonder at the daily miracles of your life, your pain would not seem less wondrous than your joy;

And you would accept the seasons of your heart, even as you have always accepted the seasons that pass over your fields.

And you would watch with serenity through the winters of your grief.

Much of your pain is self-chosen.

It is the bitter potion by which the physician within you heals your sick self.

Therefore trust the physician, and drink his remedy in silence and tranquility:

For his hand, though heavy and hard, is guided by the tender hand of the Unseen,

And the cup he brings, though it burn your lips, has been fashioned of the clay which the Potter has moistened with His own sacred tears.

—Kahlil Gibran, *The Prophet, On Pain*

An event that changed my life

— Please, tell us about a significant event that affected your life.

— *When I was ten years old, I was hit by a car. It was moving too fast, and I was moving too slow. I spent that summer in bed while all my friends played outside.*

— Was this situation unexpected?

— *Yes.*

— What state were you in before this happened? Could you have imagined that this was going to happen to you?

— *No. I vividly remember what happened ten minutes prior to it. Even now, after so many years have passed, I remember how high and bright the sun was. I remember the street I was crossing. I remember standing there waiting for the light to turn green.*

— Who else can share a significant event that happened in his life.

— *I have experienced three events that completely changed my life. The first one was living for three years with my first boyfriend. It affected everything that followed. Then, I experienced a serious disease. The last one was my moving to a new city.*

— If you had a chance to go back and to re-live it again, would you want these events to repeat themselves?

— *I would want them to happen again, but I would act differently now.*

— Did these events provide you with something that allowed you to understand yourself and other people better?

— *These events have changed me. Sometimes I wonder whether they have changed me for the best or for the worse. These were very negative events, but I am not sure whether I would want to change them or not. I don't know. If I was to experience them again, everything would probably be the same.*

— You have said that these events caused you to change significantly. What if these events did not happen? Would you not have changed or would those changes have occurred anyway? How do you relate to the changes that happened to you in connection with these events?

— *These events were necessary for these changes to occur. I would have preferred them to be less painful but equally effective. If I were to live in solitude somewhere in a desert, I would not have changed.*

— You are saying that the changes that happened to you were both good and bad. What kind of changes were they? Which of your changes do you consider to be good and which changes do you consider to be bad?

— *I am talking about changes in my point of view on life in general. I cannot say that these events were good or bad. I'd rather say they gave me something and took something away from me.*

— What exactly did they give you? Did they change your character? Did they change your perception of people and events? What exactly have these events changed in you?

— *I have started to look at life like an adult. My adolescent euphoria disappeared. Sometimes I feel sad—why did it end so fast?*

— And how do you relate to the changes that occurred in you?

— *In regards to the events that already happened, I usually think, "Whatever happened, happened." Sometimes, however, I blame these events for what is happening to me now. When I catch myself doing that, I realize that what has happened happened... Of course, I would rather that these changes had occurred in accordance to my wishes, but I don't always have enough willpower to finish what I think has to be finished.*

— Do we always know what we want to change in ourselves? Do we know what we really want or what we really don't want? Do we want the changes that happen in your life to occur the way we want them to occur? Do we really know what we want?

— *Until recently I frequently did not know what I wanted. I knew that I wanted a certain "set" that I could choose from. I can say I knew for sure what I did not want.*

"I did not want that, but I got it…"

— How often does life give you something that you don't want?

— *I have been given a serious disease to experience. It affected my life to a great degree. No one wants to be sick.*

— And why does life give us something that we don't want. We don't ask life to give it to us, but it gives it to us. Why? Does life want to treat us badly? Why does it give us ordeals such as the death of a loved one, a divorce, destruction of ideals, etc.? Why do things like that happen in our lives?

— *Life gives us what we need at the moment.*

— But do we understand that we need it?

— *No. It took me fifty years to understand that everything life gave me was necessary. I accept everything now. I don't resist anymore.*

— And how many people accept everything life gives them and understand that they are given exactly what they need?

— *Not many. I only start to understand this after some time has passed… when, after experiencing a certain event, I can look at it from a distance and, seeing what I have lost, come to understand something.*

— Can we say we can understand why life gives us one or another situation only after we experience it?

— *Yes.*

— Is there any other way? Does anyone know of any other way? For example, the death of a loved one or a disease,

"Why? Why did it happen? Why did I deserve such a punishment?"

— *I think it is very important for us not to run away when something of this nature occurs. One must experience everything to the fullest and not run way.*

— You cannot run away. It is impossible.

— *We can fool ourselves, thinking it is possible.*

— We can blame life and other people. We can try to resist change, but that will not lead us anywhere. These situations will not disappear. On the contrary, they will get worse. Look at the man who doesn't accept his disease. He yells and screams. He blames everyone around him. Can he get better while behaving this way?

And what about a man who accepts what happens to him, a disease with a poor prognosis or some other serious challenge? He might not understand why he was dealt such a card, but he accepts it, understanding that by going through this ordeal he may understand something very important.

Take people infected with HIV, for example. Many people did not understand what was happening to them. Their friends and relatives would avoid them. Some of them accepted the disease and by going through it understood something very important. Their relationship with life changed in the process of experiencing that serious illness. Many of them knew they would not survive for long, and they spent their last days in a very unusual way. Many of them said at the end that they understood things they would have never understood were they to not meet this calamity. Their friends' attitudes toward them, as well as their own attitudes toward the people around them, underwent tremendous changes.

And what about people who are diagnosed with cancer and know that their chances of survival are very low? These diseases help many people understand something they cannot understand in any other way. Some of these people have described what happens to them as horrible and beautiful at the same time. Some of them have come to understand themselves only through the disease. They were able to see something that was hidden from them before. Many of them forgave the people they were upset with only because of this serious challenge. Their relatives' attitudes toward them changed after their death. They did not understand them when they were alive. They blamed, argued, and feuded with them. But now, after their passing, they see their relationship in a totally different light. What they could not understand before suddenly became clear. Perhaps it could not have happened any other way. Some people are unable to understand anything even after going through such an ordeal. Life provides everyone with an opportunity to find something very important in these difficult situations. People are not the same afterwards. Perhaps they didn't want to change, but life forced them to do that.

In essence, life consists of constant transformation, movement, and flow. Most people want stability. They want to create their own world where everything has a place, where there are no surprises, and everything is the way they want it to be. Do you know anyone who was able to create such a world and maintain it for long?

— *One can create such a world, but it will not be permanent. Sooner or later life will interfere with it. Something will happen, and it may be destroyed.*

Neither dead nor alive

— I have not met a man who was able to create his own world, which life, in all its power and glory, did not burst into at one point or another. It sometimes bursts in a completely unexpected way, like a river overflowing its banks. People scream, "Why? Why me? I just want everything to be the way it was! But life bursts in and destroys everything they have built. Have you experienced this? Even now, when I ask you this question, you are afraid of changes. You don't want to reply. You want to wait it out. Perhaps it will not get to me. Perhaps it will choose someone else. That is not going to happen. I am the surprise that will burst into your steady, habitual life. You think, "No. This will not touch me." This is your life position. That's why, for most people, change represents something horrible. They are not ready for it and do not want to prepare for it. Yet for some people, life is beautiful just because they are always ready to change. They are waiting for change, and they are not afraid of it. For them, everything life brings is great. They expect change all the time. Thus, change does not destroy them. Change destroys those who are afraid of it. People are usually not afraid of external changes. They are afraid of inner changes. Many don't want to change and continue to hold onto their old, habitual selves. By doing that, they go against the basic law of life. This law, which many people have unfortunately forgotten, is the law of self-knowledge. And until a human being understands that self-knowledge is the major stimulus of life, he will neither be dead nor alive. Life does not tolerate that. It will change and transform him, or it will break him, forcing him to change. No one here can avoid change.

So, how do you perceive the changes in your life? Are you ready for them or do you think they will not affect you? What does Russia experience now? The country is going through some serious changes. No one will be able to escape them. Some people will try to hide, but they will not succeed. Change will catch up with everyone one way or another. So, you'd better get out and meet it face to face. Some soldiers die with bullets in their backs. Many die with bullets in their chests. Yet others don't die because they are not afraid.

— *I have experienced a serious change in my life, but I am not sure I want to talk about it.*

— This is your right. You don't have to talk about it.

— *This was the most serious change I have experienced over the last five years, but I don't want to talk about it.*

— Some people collect changes the way others collect empty bottles.

— *I don't want to collect them like empty bottles…*

— **When a man talks about something, he starts to see it from another side. When he honestly speaks about it, he has an opportunity to really understand what is happening to him. Perhaps that explains the strong necessity of people who have experienced stressful, dramatic situations to share their experiences with others. They search for someone with whom to discuss and to share their experience. Perhaps behind it is a subconscious desire to take a different look at what happened to them and to understand what it was.**

— *I have already discussed it.*

— I am not asking you to discuss it now.

— *I cannot remember any other changes now.*

— Okay. What kind of changes have you experienced over the last twelve months?

201

— I started to attend your school last year. Since then, my outlook on life has changed. I found new friends here. Even my character has changed.

— Did the changes you experienced appear on their own or did you create them yourself?

— I have created them myself.

— How did you create them?

— I don't know.

— How can you create something and not know how you did it? Who do you want to become? Many people experience change. When something they call bad happens to them, they feel disappointed. When something that they call good happens to them, they feel happy. But everything that happens to them just happens, irrespective of whether they consider it to be good or bad. It just happens. They flatter themselves with the idea that they do it themselves, but in reality, what happens to them just happens to them. Why does it happen to them? Perhaps it happens so they will understand something? And when they understand it, they will see life the way it really is.

Recently, many people lost their jobs. This process continues, and it will escalate. Many people were sitting in their corporations on their behinds doing nothing. They blamed everyone and everything for their life, but they did not make any effort to improve their situation until they were laid off. Now, they scream that they cannot find a job. They could have predicted their situation, but they did not. They are more comfortable pretending that nothing has happened. If they wanted to, they could have seen it coming years before the crash. But they did not do anything to find another job. They were stagnating there. They stopped evolving, and their companies deteriorated. Perhaps they should have thought about what they wanted from their job a long time ago. Did they? No. Most people don't do that. As a result, they get laid off. They cannot find a job for a long time. They start to pity themselves, and they get sick. This is a typical scenario.

Do you feel where your life circumstances are pointing you? Do you take any steps to correct the situation, or do you simply wait to be fired or laid off?

"I used to think I accept everything..."

— *I have witnessed some horrific events during my life. I have seen people experience terrible physical and emotional pain. I knew that their suffering was not coincidental.*

But what should I do when the man next to me is being beaten to death or when I see someone bleeding to death? Something happens to this man, but I cannot do anything... I don't even know what I should do. I have witnessed many such incidents. The last time something of this nature happened to me, I was able to understand why I met this man. Before I've met him, I used to think I was accepting of everything. And then I experienced things with him that I don't even want to describe. These were hard things for me to witness.

When I see a man who is suffering, I understand that at this point of his life he must experience the ordeal he experiences. Mentally I understand that, but I don't understand why he must experience it in such a harsh way. It seems to be very cruel. Mentally I understand that he must experience it, but I cannot accept it. I thought I accepted everything, but after what has happened, I realize that this is not the case.

— There are people around you. Some are close to you and some are distant. All of them suffer one way or another. Whatever happens to them is related to you personally. You can say that you don't expect anything from life anymore. That's what many people say. But there are people next to you. Something happens to them, and it affects you. If someone

203

next to you says that he does not care about himself, he nevertheless feels for those who are next to him. When people who are close to you, your friends and relatives, start to feel bad, they ask you why it is happening to them. Even if they don't ask you this question directly, you can see this question in their eyes. To continue to think that this has nothing to do with you, while looking into their eyes and seeing their pain, is to fool yourself. Someone will get into an accident. Another will get sick. Does this happen to the people who are close to you? Why does it happen? Why did a man live for thirty years and suddenly get into an accident? Why is he in a hospital? Why are the doctors not sure whether he will walk or not? Why? What is this? Is this his punishment? But if this is punishment, it is a punishment for the people who are close to him too. Why does life treat us in such a way? Have any one of you asked this question? How did you answer it? What if such a man were to come and ask you, "Why did this happen to me?" What would you tell him? Perhaps, you would say, "It's life. Things happen. Calm down. Take a pill. It will pass." That's what many people say, but that cannot solve anything. So, what are we left with? Someone may reach a conclusion that life consists of constant suffering, everything around him is horrible, and he is lucky he is not dead yet. But why did it happen to you? Is it a coincidence? But even if this is a coincidence, why did it happen to you?

— *We can only understand what has happened to us after we have experienced it. I can perceive the events that happened to me from different levels now. As more time elapses, I can perceive more and more of it. First, you think that it was given to you for one thing. Then you start to perceive it deeper. I am experiencing certain changes now. Looking back at my life, I can say I did not plan many of the events that happened to me. They have happened spontaneously. I perceived them primarily on the material level. Now, however, my perception has changed to such a degree that the habitual picture of the world has been broken. I have always thought I could accept everything, but I can see now that I am still afraid of many things.*

— Let's say something happens to a human being that he cannot accept. Does the event itself continue to occur or does it disappear?

— *It continues to occur.*

— Do you think it will continue to occur for a long time? How long will the changes occur if you don't accept them?

— *It seems to me, they can continue for a long time, and if one tries to avoid them, they can come in a different form later on.*

— *Can I ask you a question, Alexander Alexandrovich? What happens to people who get killed during wars? What do they understand before they die?*

— Every human being understands what he is ready to understand. Sudden death is not the most favorable way to exit this reality from the point of view of awareness, i.e. one's pursuit of becoming aware of oneself. People used to prepare for death in the past. The same can be said about birth. Some people prepare themselves to give an "aware birth." This is very important. When two human beings conceive in a state of alcohol intoxication, they should expect to deliver a child affected by alcohol. If, however, they understand that this is one of the most important events of their life and prepare for it, a brighter and more advanced Soul enters the body of their child. If a man, knowing that he is about to die, prepares for his death, his transition to another world will be totally different from the transition of one who happens to be in an unaware state at the moment of death. Some people feel that they are about to die, but do not prepare themselves, and continue to remain in the usual for them state of "waking sleep." Everything depends on the way a man prepares for his death. What does he think? How does he relate to it? Everything in human life is an opportunity. Some of us use these opportunities, while others don't even see them.

I cannot answer your question, "What does a man experience who dies suddenly?" in any concrete way. Different people experience different things, but the occurrence of a sudden, unexpected death probably tells us that this human being did not consider death to be an event he had to prepare for and meet in full awareness.

— *But life does not end with death. He will be reborn again, and he will experience everything again. Isn't it so?*

"After the doctor left, I understood I was dying…"

— Those who know this truth are not here. Those who are here now do not know it.

— *A few years ago, I almost died. I was diagnosed with neuralgia at ten o'clock in the morning. Four hours later, I understood that I was dying. It turned out that I had severe pneumonia. I spent five days in ICU. I was lucky. I was in the hands of good doctors. They spent hours pressing on my chest, trying to bring me back. At that point, I realized that the last thing that gets turned off during death is the sense of hearing. It is also the first sense to get turned on. I was gone already when suddenly my hearing returned, and I heard one doctor saying to another, "Keep going! She is going to make it!" The other one screamed back, "What are you talking about?! She does not have a pulse. She is not breathing. Her blood pressure is zero. She is gone." I heard "morgue" in my head, but I could not say anything because I was already gone; my ears heard, but I didn't see anything and I could not move my tongue. I would return from time to time. I had just one thought in my head: "You are an idiot! Look*

206

*what you did to yourself. Your young son is going to be an orphan now."
Afterwards, I started to love myself. Has anyone here had a near death
experience?*

— *My experience was different. I did not have to go to a hospital. I
was not sick. I experienced a situation a year ago, when I suddenly felt
that I had died. This sensation was so strong that all my friends and
relatives were telling me that I looked like a dead man, and I really felt
that way. I was looking at people, and I understood everything they did
and said, but at the same time, I was on the other side. I was not in this
world. I was looking at everything as if from the outside. I understood a
lot. Slowly, I started to return to life. Everything changed in my life
afterwards. That was my near-death experience. I was walking and
something was happening to me; I felt how consciousness turned on, how
the heart started to work, how my hands and feet got warmer. I was slowly
coming back to life. I have experienced daily changes since then. I do not
divide the events of my life into significant and insignificant. Getting to see
a sunset or a flower blooming is an important event for me. Everything is
very important for me now. In comparison with that nowhere state, I just
feel what it means to be alive.*

— We have already discussed that a human being starts to
really understand life only when he gets closer to his
understanding of death. This not only happens through NDE.
This can happen, for example, when you experience the death
of someone who is close to you. In my case, that happened
after I had experienced the death of my grandmother and my
parents. I perceived their deaths as a chain of events, which
were accompanied by very strong emotional states. I have **felt
and experienced** the deaths of my loved ones. We could say
that during that time, I died three times. Afterwards, I had
other experiences. I experienced my own death. It is precisely
these experiences of death that gave me an understanding of
what life really is. Through these experiences, I started to

understand myself. My first reaction to my grandmother's death was manifested by an unexplained necessity to run. I loved her dearly, and she loved me. I was heavily into sports back then, and the only way I could handle it was to run. I used to run and talk to myself. I would tell myself that life is beautiful. Some information about death and NDE experience can be found in my early books. Moody's *Life after Death* is one of the best books on the subject. He speaks of the fact that a man does not die after life leaves his body. Something remains, and this something sees and hears. It finds itself in another, completely different world inhabited by unfamiliar creatures. Everything is different there. You can read these books and watch movies related to this topic, but this is just information. You can agree or disagree with this information. Perhaps some of you will find it interesting, but the way I see it, the only thing that can convert information into understanding are your own personal experiences. My personal experience brought me to understand that our true "I" is clear consciousness, the nature of which is eternity. Clear consciousness can enter and exit any form and any body. In this physical world—the world of forms—people cling to and try to hold onto things that are of no importance within the spheres of clear awareness. It is the level of your awareness that determines where you will transfer to after the death of your physical body. Your consciousness will be attracted to the spheres that correspond to the level of your awareness. If you are attracted by illusions, you will return to the world of illusions again. This will continue until you decide to see life the way it really is, i.e. to see reality. Life in the physical body is given to us so we can see false as false and approach the real perception of the world as closely as possible, because reality removes every mask of illusion. At the moment of death, the consciousness of a human being separates from the habitual illusions, dependencies, and false attachments. But you can feel scared seeing reality, because you got used to seeing only the illusions. In that case, you would be seduced by the world of illusions again. If you have not finished something here or have not accepted someone here, you will not be able to do it after death. To accept and to take a step toward another human being, you need to change yourself and your perception of what happens around you. You can start to see reality without parting with your body. That's where our way of self-understanding and self-awareness leads. Stop spending energy on the unreal, illusory things. The changes that life offers us here, sometimes in a very dramatic form, carry great opportunities that can help us understand our true nature.

Life only takes away false things

— I want to add something to the topic of illusory things people pursue in life. A year ago, I experienced a situation that shocked me. One of my friends used to love his apartment pathologically. He furnished it with the most expensive furniture and the best stereo system money could buy. He was spending enormous amount of time and money on its upkeep. And then one day, he was robbed. He cried, "They did not just rob me of some things. They stole a piece of my life." When we became aware of the situation, we got scared.

— Yes, life usually strips a man of precisely what he considers to be himself, i.e. with what he identifies himself. Your friend is not what he lost. Nothing he has ever lost, loses, or may lose is him. However, many people identify themselves with wealth, power, pleasure, or with another human being. When they are deprived of their identification, they get into a state of shock. They experience it as if part of their life was taken away from them. But even though many of you think that way, you are, in reality, neither money nor power. Everything false and illusory that we consider to be ourselves or our life can and will be taken away from us so we can find out who we really are. When life takes something false away from us, we experience shock. Some people, in coming out of this shock, resume their behavior and start to accumulate wealth, power, and pleasure until they are taken away from them again. Why are these things taken away from them? They are taken away from them so they can understand that they are not all these things, they are something else. If a man cannot understand himself, everything false he has accumulated will be taken away from him again and again. He will continue to place blame and be at a loss as to why this is happening to him. However, there are people who, while going through change and dramatic situations in their life, start to understand themselves. Some do it slower, while others do it faster. They start to see that what they were trying to grab on to throughout their lifetime is not them. In this case, the changes that they have experienced transform from misfortunes into blessings. Some schools of thought say that everything that happens to us is a retribution for our sins. In a way, this is true. But the sin is in man's not understanding who he really is. A man does not understand who he is and as a result pursues something ephemeral, something that is not him, insisting on his illusory perception of the world. This is the only "sin" worthy of discussion. As you can see, this is not what people usually mean when they talk about sins. The death of the physical body is a moment of liberation, the moment we part with the illusions we have accumulated throughout our lifetime. If all a man did during his life was to accumulate illusions, this moment will be a great shock for him. But if, throughout his life, a man could understand more and more who he really is, this last transfer of a given life would be totally different. Perhaps it would be one of the greatest experiences of his life.

No one can escape this transfer. Everything that happens to people throughout their lives can be seen as a preparation for this last transfer. But how many people understand why they experience dramatic changes in their life? How many people understand that every ordeal they experience is related to the preparation we are discussing? Do they treat them as a preparation for their last transfer or continue to misunderstand, get upset, and hate? Which direction do they move toward? Any situation can turn into a big opportunity, but some will extract something very important from this opportunity, while others will not get anything out of it. How do you treat the opportunities life offers you? The lessons that life offers to people are very different. If you are a feeling man who understands things, you may only require a gentle tap on the shoulder to guide you toward necessary self-changes. But if you are a callous brute who doesn't understand anything, life has no other choice but to kick you hard. If you don't understand that either, the "dose" will be escalated. Diseases, traumas, and accidents are the extreme lessons for those who continue to persist in their not understanding. When one cannot understand his lesson in a gentle form, life must explain itself in a harsh form. What else can life do to motivate a man to start thinking? Everyone must go through his lessons on his own, and life offers the best opportunity to do it. Our daily life is a chain of such opportunities. It is precisely how the life of a human being differs from the life of animals, plants, and minerals, who do not have this opportunity to understand and to become aware of themselves. Why do we consider a human being to be a godlike creature? We do that because he has an opportunity to become aware of himself and of the world. It is precisely in awareness, not in simple intellectualization, where his godlike essence manifests itself. But what does a human being do? Does he use this opportunity, or does he prefer to return to the animal, plant, or mineral kingdom? No one has the right to force a human being to do anything. Life can provide a man with an opportunity, but how he uses it depends on him and him alone.

— *It seems to me, there are no opportunities here. I have always tried to get a job and to make some money. I fought and tried to resist the fact that I was without a job. And then, one day, I realized that I don't need it. Everything I did was working against what I really needed. Money would come on its own when I needed it. I would borrow money when I needed money. Then I would find some kind of work that would allow me to pay back what I owed, no more and no less. I stopped fighting it. I started to understand that this is how it should be, and that I cannot change it.*

— What exactly do you think "should be"?

— *The formation of a human being here on Earth and his preparation for this transfer that you have discussed is what should be.*

— And how does this formation occur? Doesn't it require one to apply some effort? Based on your story, I understood that you tried to apply some effort but then decided that you did not need to do that.

Can one find who he is without doing anything?

— *I started to think that I was not doing what I was supposed to be doing.*

— And what are you supposed to be doing?

— *Well, first of all, I need to find out who I am and why I am here.*

— Can a man find out who he is by not doing anything? Many people believe that in order to get to know themselves, they have to abandon ordinary life and regular activities. Many sects and some orthodox monasteries still operate based on this notion, but this is not a viable option today. This was necessary at a certain period of our development, but many things have changed since then. A human being is not born among similar human beings to separate himself from them and to spend his life in a monastery. And if we want to get to know ourselves without moving away from people, we need to do something. You came here to get to know yourself through your actions and relationships. It is important for you to get to know yourself, because unless you know who you are, you will not be able to find out what you need to do. But you can only understand this by acting in this physical world. In other words, you start to do things not because you owe something to someone but because you understand what your main assignment is. By doing that, you change something in this world. One must understand who he really is in order to have wisdom and power to do what he needs to do in this world. Many people say that there is a lot of injustice, wrong doing, and fear in this world. You frequently encounter these discussions when you read newspapers, listen to the radio, or watch television. We are being presented this as a certain fact. Have you thought about your own role in all of this? Perhaps you are afraid of your own fear and don't want to change anything. Do you even understand that this can be changed, that it has to change? Perhaps you don't understand how it can be changed or think it is impossible to change anything here.

— *A man must have the strength to change himself.*

— Where will you get this strength? Who will give it to you?

— *You have said that when a man comes to know himself, he gets stronger. When he comes to know himself completely, he starts to act. He can affect the society that surrounds him to a certain degree, but until that moment his effect on it is negligible.*

— A man who does nothing will never understand himself. A man who does nothing will see himself as a small leaf falling off a tree, a leaf that does not know where the wind will take it. How can he understand himself if he does not do anything? A man starts to understand himself only by living within society where he does things and interacts with other people. That's when he starts to understand himself. As his understanding grows, his inner power increases. He starts to see what he does and begins to do things better. This vision only comes to someone who does something. The one who does nothing will not be able to see anything. Such a man will see the chain of life events as nothing but coincidences.

It is not coincidental that our Process has started in Russia, the place where East meets West. There are different ways to understand oneself. In the East, many people follow the way of meditation, during which a man just sits in solitude. However, there are other ways for man to understand himself. Perhaps the middle way, which offers this understanding while a man interacts with other people, suits the Western man better. Perhaps both ways are necessary, and perhaps here, in Russia, we have the opportunity to connect these two ways and understand ourselves better. Perhaps at this stage of the evolution of humanity, we need to connect our feminine side, which is strongly developed in the East, with our masculine side, which is strongly developed in the West.

Where do I get the power to live?

— I would like to say something in connection to what Andrey was saying. Where would this power come from? When I interact with people, I experience certain thoughts, feelings, emotions, and sensations. I try to track them down. I **observe** *them. They get stronger because I pay attention to them. As soon as they become visible, what I really need starts to blossom like a flower, and what I don't need does not tolerate my undivided attention but gets smaller and leaves. It is important not just to go under the girdle of what you feel or sense but to pay attention to it and to track it down. Perhaps that is where one can get the strength.*

— Many people spend a lot of energy trying to understand what is right and what is wrong, what they should do and what they should not do, what is good in them and what is bad in them. Those are the questions that bother people. There is one simple and universal way to answer these questions. **It is a way of awareness.** When a human being starts to become aware of himself, i.e. of his thoughts, feelings, and actions, what is right for him stays with him, and what is wrong for him leaves him.

A human being who starts to become aware of himself, starts to understand more and more and to become who he really is. You don't need to go to the Himalayas. You don't need to study philosophical systems or moral codes. You just need to be aware of yourself. Are you aware of everything that happens in your inner world? What kind of thoughts do you harbor there? What kinds of feelings do you harbor there? How do you realize them? Awareness provides you with an opportunity to investigate and to understand yourself. You will see how a thought brings in a feeling, and how feeling leads to action. You will not do the things that are currently leading you astray. You will avoid the tragic events that could have happened to you had you not been aware of yourself.

— *What forces people to search for awareness, Alexander Alexandrovich? I think most people start to search for awareness only to look at other people from above and say, "I am aware of everything! You are not aware of anything."*

— The one who says that cannot be aware. This can only be said by a man who explains things. When something happens to a human being, something that forces him to part with what's habitual for him though he does not want to part with it, he thinks up multiple explanations to justify his desires. One can explain everything if he really wants to.

— *Are you saying that a human being is interested in explanations that would allow him to explain his desires?*

— That's what most people are occupied with. They don't want to change themselves. But something happens to them, and they start to doubt the correctness of their actions. They either need to change, or they need to reinforce the strategy that justifies them. In either case, they bring up and use different philosophical, moral, and psychological theories to explain why everything they do is correct, and why they need to continue to do what they are in the habit of doing.

— *You are right. It is extremely difficult for me to not justify myself and to become aware of myself. Most of the time, I am moved by the search for theory that has the words "The Truth" written on it; only rarely do I become aware of myself. It is difficult to walk the walk of awareness.*

— Someone got used to doing something a certain way. Let's say a man was fighting in a war, and he got used to killing people. Back home after the war, he does not think why he had to take the lives of other people. He starts to search for people who did what he did and tries to understand how they explain it. When he finds these people, he accepts their explanations, and quite frequently he continues to do what he is in the habit of doing, i.e. to kill.

— *Yes. It appears to be very easy. Just drop all philosophical concepts and live, simply live. But in that case, you submerge into this life even more, which, as it appears to me, is quite scary and much more difficult than any philosophical theory.*

— Life cannot be expressed by philosophical theories. Life is so great that no one can force it into any boundaries. Any such an attempt is doomed to fail. Any new philosophical, psychological, or religious theory can carry kernels of truth, but in the end, even they get lost behind all the words and explanations which are usually introduced into any theory. No one can explain life. One should live it, and one should live it in a state of awareness. This is not easy because a human being is taught to see everything upside down. It is difficult work to live in a state of awareness, but it is the only way to understand what really makes you happy and what makes you unhappy. There is no other way. And if people do something that makes them unhappy, they do it not because they want to do it, but because they are mistaken, i.e. not aware of themselves. If a man gets hit on the head by stepping on the same rake for the hundredth time, he probably does not understand that it is precisely his habitual actions that led him to step on it. He just does not see it. Thus, he continues to do what he has always done. If a man screams, yells, hits, and kills another man, he does it only because he does not understand what he is really doing. He puts his hand into the fire and gets burned by it because he does not understand what he is doing. He can only understand what he is doing by becoming aware. If a man were to do what he usually did in a state of awareness, whatever he does not need would simply leave him. Most people don't want to change anything in their life. They want to continue to do what they have always done. They don't strive toward awareness. They don't want to experience inner change. But you will not be able to protect yourself from the events that will change your life. You will encounter them regardless of whether you want them or not. For example, a man who fools people and steals from them will, eventually, experience what they experience. He can claim it to be an accident and blame it on a mistake he had made. He can promise himself to be more vigilant next time, but he will be fooled and robbed again. Soon he will not be able to avoid this karmic return. The same thing will happen to him repeatedly, but he will not understand it because he is not ready to become aware of himself. That's the reason he cannot understand what is really happening to him.

A popular misunderstanding—I will change myself through others

— *I noticed that many people who insist they want to change themselves frequently don't want to do that. In reality, they want to change other people. They find fault in their friends and neighbors and start to explain to them what they are doing wrong. They insist they want to get to know themselves, but they don't. They don't even see themselves. You said that life cannot be explained, but I will say that life is love. When you really love, you love yourself and others irrespective of what gender or nationality they are. When you love, you understand what life is really about, even if you can't explain it in words.*

— Those who understand will understand you. But they must understand it not by reading about it in books. We can't say that people don't know about this. Many things we discuss are written in the Bible. Many people have read it and know it, but do they feel it?

— *When a man starts to look inside himself and to change himself, something really starts to happen.*

— A human being is the way he is, and whatever he can become depends on him. Once he starts to understand that, he starts to create specific situations to accelerate his evolution. If he doesn't understand that, he tries to push these situations away. Every one of us is the way he is at a given moment, but who do we want to become? Who do you want to be a year from now?

— *I want to better understand what is happening around me.*

— *You may laugh, but I want to be happier.*

— *I want to be more decisive.*

— *I want to be healthy, calm, and beautiful.*

— *I want to get to know myself better, and I want to get rid of my complexes.*

— *I want to get rid of the notions I inherited because they interfere with my life. I don't want to react to opinions of other people. I want to be able to hear people and not feel anything.*

— Do you want to die?

— *No, I just don't want to depend on the opinions of others.*

— You've said you don't want to feel anything. A dead man does not feel anything.

— *I have not expressed myself properly. I don't want to react …*

— A dead man does not react to anything.

— *Then I want to be dead.*

— So you will have a funeral pretty soon. Will you invite us?

— *I invite all of you.*

— Great. We have been invited to a funeral.

— *I want to stop worrying, and I want my mind to stop appraising me.*

— *I want to learn how to love …*

— Yes, nothing can be simpler. We all know that we cannot receive anything in this world for free. We must pay for everything. How will you pay for what you want to receive? What are you ready to sacrifice?

A and B were sitting on the pipe …

— *I am ready to sacrifice my egoism for love.*

— *I am ready to sacrifice the suffering I will have to experience to get there.*

— *I am ready to sacrifice my irritability.*

— *I don't know. I am ready to sacrifice whatever must be sacrificed for it.*

— What would be the most difficult for you to part with?

— *It is probably my body that I will have most difficult time sacrificing. I don't think I am ready for it.*

— And how will you realize the advantages you will receive if you were to sacrifice your body?

— *What do I need my body for if I am free and fearless?*

— And who is it that is going to be free and fearless?

— *My spirit.*

— But your spirit is presently in your body.

— *Yes, it is still there.*

— Have you decided to free it from this extra weight?

— *I would want to collect all my inner parts, the parts that tear me to pieces, and to figure out what I really want. I can sacrifice anything. This part is easy.*

— Are you saying it is easy to sacrifice? Do you know what exactly you will have to sacrifice to collect all your inner "i"s together?

— *I don't know.*

— Perhaps you will need to sacrifice exactly these "i"s.

220

— *But something has to be left?*

— And for which "i" will you sacrifice all other "i"s for? They scream and fight now because they exist. What will happen when they disappear?

— *Let me put it differently. I don't want to get all of them together. I want to get to the place from which all of them originated. Perhaps they will all fall away.*

— Are you ready to sacrifice the desires of all these multiple "i"s?

— *Yes.*

— Which particular desire of yours are you ready to sacrifice? It is easy to say that you can sacrifice everything, but most people find it difficult to sacrifice something specific.

— *I don't know. I constantly want something new.*

— What do you want now?

— *I want to eat.*

— Do you want to have a big, delicious meal?

— *Well, I can have a small one.*

— Are you ready to sacrifice it?

— *I can sacrifice it for a certain period of time.*

— That's why it is so difficult to change! We want to get something new without parting with the old. Moreover, what we want is usually completely opposite to what we have; we hope to keep what we have and to get something new. The tragedy of a human being is in his desire to get something new without parting with the old. His entire room is filled with the old furniture. He wants to buy a new set of furniture, and at the same time, he does not want to part with the old furniture. That's exactly what happens in the inner world of a human being. I want to be noble, but I don't want to part with my greediness. I will be both noble and greedy. Is that possible? No. But a man continues to believe that this is possible. In this

221

case, nothing will change, but a man continues to flatter himself with the illusion that something will change in him: "I am getting enlightened." He was asleep, and he remains asleep.

— *I am observing something very interesting now. I am out of questions. I used to ask myself multiple questions before: "Why? How? What's the reason for that?" I don't have any questions now.*

— What do you have then?

— *Only the answers.*

— A and B were sitting on a pipe. A fell off, and B disappeared. Who is sitting on the pipe?

*   *   *

9781944722043